Harbor Voices

Rounding the mark near Newark Bay's Port Newark–Elizabeth Marine Terminal, the Bayonne Bridge well astern. . . . Container ship outward bound in Kill Van Kull, between Staten Island, NY, and Bayonne, NJ.

Merry Christmas to Hunt 2008 - from Dad & Ethel

Harbor Voices

New York Harbor tugs, ferries, people, places, & more . . .

To Hunt Stehli —

Terry Walton

12/3/08

Anthology by Terry Walton

Sea History Press • National Maritime Historical Society

With Thanks

We are grateful for leadership gifts from the J. Aron Charitable Foundation,
Furthermore, a program of the J. M. Kaplan Fund,
the New York City Environmental Fund of the Hudson River Foundation,
the James A. Macdonald Foundation,
the Marine Society of the City of New York,
and the Ann Eden Woodward Foundation,
and also for generous gifts from Bronson Binger, Pien and Hans Bosch,
Queene Hooper Foster, Howard Slotnick, and Robert Hussey.

Seaport magazine and South Street *Reporter* articles,
copyright © South Street Seaport Museum, reprinted with permission.
Copyright © National Maritime Historical Society 2008
5 John Walsh Boulevard, PO Box 68, Peekskill, NY 10566
914-737-7878 • www.seahistory.org • nmhs@seahistory.org
ISBN: 978-0-930248-14-7
Design by Inger Gibb
Production by Rosalie Ink Publications, RosalieInk.com
Printing by Avon Press, Hauppauge, NY

Acknowledgements

The *Harbor Voices* anthology is the work of many hands, devoted ones all. Peter Stanford, founder of South Street Seaport Museum with his wife Norma, and today editor-at-large of NMHS's *Sea History* magazine, suggested the title. Ship historian Norman Brouwer – my co-adventurer for harbor explorations for the Museum's *Seaport* magazine, helped select favorite articles for reprinting here and reviewed the outcome. Museum director Mary Pelzer welcomed the whole idea and waived reprint fees as she encouraged our work. *Seaport* magazine photographers – reached years after we had first known each other – joined Mary in their generous permissions. Capt. John Doswell of the Working Harbor Committee reviewed all and responded swiftly with hours of harbor-knowledge help. Harbor photographer Bernard Ente said yes to my every plea for his spectacular photographs. Designer Inger Gibb created handsome pages with a glad and resilient heart. Burchenal Green and Ron Oswald of National Maritime Historical Society said enthusiastic yes when invited to serve as publisher. And as for funding, Joan Davidson, Peter Aron, Walter Handelman, and Pat Woods were lead supporters – encouraging others to help us meet our budget. ★ Art and scans from Museum files are the early and generous work of Jeff Remling and Richard Stepler. I welcomed research and other guidance from Sara Appman, Steven Bendo, Cindy Collins, Jan Eisenman, Lee Gruzen, Karen Kennedy, Sue Lathrop, Virginia Perkins, Elizabeth Powers, Alison Simko, Jennifer Stanley, Jeanie Tengelsen, Liz Watson, and Marcia Wiley. New writings are the gift of Jonathan Atkin, Bill Bleyer, Norman Brouwer, John Doswell, David Fuchs, Hope Killcoyne, John Mylod, Sarina Shef, Richard Stepler, and Jenifer Walton, with logistical help from Kaitlyn Pawlukojc, Susan Schaefer, and John Titus. Throughout, cheerings-on came from the abovementioned all, and from Lucy Ambrosino of the Port Authority of NY/NJ, Bill Baker of Channel Thirteen, Kent Barwick of the Municipal Art Society, Meg Black and the Working Harbor Committee, Capt. Huntley Gill of fireboat *John J. Harvey*, Capt. Pamela Hepburn of tug *Pegasus*, artist Naima Rauam, and Erin Urban of Noble Maritime Collection. ★ In all, it is the gifts of knowledge, writing, art, permissions, fees generously waived, and encouragement freely given that I here gratefully acknowledge. TW

To
Seaman Henry Slack, New York Naval Militia, 1898
Ltjg Henry Campbell Slack, USCG
Henry Campbell Slack Jr.
Capt. Frank Ley
Robert Prentiss Walton
– Sailors all

Chart detail, berths of *U.S.S. Granite State* and *Tusitala*, NY harbor.

Square-rigger *Tusitala*, Ltjg Henry Slack, USCG, & Capt. Frank Ley, NY harbor.

NY Naval Militia Training Ship *U.S.S. Granite State*, Seaman Henry Slack, NY harbor c 1898.

Preface

New York harbor has always inspired people with the long, long thoughts of youth, their eyes fixed on far horizons. It has engaged old timers in re-telling seamen's yarns and artists seeking the new perspectives which open up as city buildings dwindle away like palings in a fence. It is the city's great connection to the wider world, as most New Yorkers are at least somewhat aware. But it is also a world of its own, and it is that world Terry Walton invites you to explore with her in *Harbor Voices*, in which harbor people tell their own stories of their experience in the great commons of the harbor.

I believe there is a harbor ethos, which turns up in fierce loyalties to fellow workers engaged in the unending and demanding business of handling ships and cargoes. There is equally fierce competition, always tempered by a constant, passionate commitment to doing things the right way. All acts have consequences, moving heavy things in narrow waters.

The great artist of the harbor is John Noble, whose work can be found everywhere in shipping offices and seamen's bars. On his death in 1983, for various reasons it fell to me to make the calls to summon harbor craft in a memorial procession in John's honor. Quick calls, no ceremony, and the boats came, rival tugboats, police boats, Sandy Hook Pilots, the lot. This was the harbor ethos at work, recognizing one of their own – like Conrad's Lord Jim, John was "one of us." There is no greater honor I can imagine.

Ms Walton's own career has taken her on a remarkable series of adventures in harbor waters and with harbor people, as a founder of the South Street Seaport Museum years ago and current vice chair of the Working Harbor Committee. Joining her on her waterborne perambulations through the wide expanses and hidden corners of the harbor, you will rejoice in the company of people who live their work completely and take great joy in it.

– Peter Stanford, President Emeritus
National Maritime Historical Society

New-York and Brooklyn Ferry.

SUCH persons as are inclined to compound,
agreeable to law, in the Steam Ferry-Boat,
Barges, or common Horse Boats, will be pleased to apply to the subscribers, who are authori-
zed to settle the same.

GEORGE HICKS, Brooklyn,
JOHN PINTARD, 52 Wall st.

Commutation for a single person not
transferable, for 12 months, $10 00
Do.   do.   8 months,   6 67

May 3, 1814   6m.

Crossing Brooklyn Ferry

"Just as you feel when you look on the river and sky, so I felt,
Just as any of you is one of a living crowd, I was one of a crowd,
Just as you are refresh'd by the gladness of the river and
*   the bright flow, I was refresh'd,*
Just as you stand and lean on the rail, yet hurry with the
*   swift current, I stood yet was hurried,*
Just as you look on the numberless masts of ships and the
*   thick-stemm'd pipes of steamboats, I look'd."*

– Walt Whitman, on the East River waters
between Manhattan and Fulton Street Brooklyn,
from "Crossing Brooklyn Ferry," *Leaves of Grass* (1891-1892)

Contents

Introduction

New York harbor really needs no introduction. For everyone knows it some, whether directly – as tug skipper or ferry passenger or water-gazer from miles of shores, or indirectly – as wearer of shoes that came in by ship, or city dweller familiar with bridges and cross-river vistas. Or, as visitor who can hardly believe his eyes at all the ever-changing action of vessel, water, people, and light.

I've loved New York harbor and gone adventuring on it for exactly forty-two years, not counting childhood commutes from New Jersey on the Hoboken ferry. But nobody knows everything about this intricate city waterway. *Harbor Voices* is my own collection of stories about harbor people, places, and vessels – inviting you to delve into harbor facets that are rich in recent memory, or present today and likely metamorphosed by tomorrow, or even this afternoon, as written about by many who love this harbor of ours. . . .

The fact is, New York is "a city built from the sea," as South Street Seaport Museum founder Peter Stanford has observed. Its shores and waters are endlessly changing and always have been, from the catastrophic glacial flood that created the Verrazano Narrows and thus superb harbor shelter for ships, from early ferries, sloops, and schooners to today's huge container-laden vessels filled with cocoa and televisions and every other imaginable item heading in for inland shops or out to distant ports. Then there's Newtown Creek in Queens, the Atlantic and Erie basins in Brooklyn, Staten Island's bordering waterway Kill Van Kull, all explorable on harbor tours today and touched upon in *Harbor Voices*. Plus New Jersey's giant-size Colgate clock and parks and palisades, not to mention Lower Manhattan's diminutive Fireboat Pier A (my favorite waterfront structure), the Hudson piers with refurbishings well underway, and East River traffic braving the chaotic waters of Hell Gate en route to Long Island Sound. *Harbor Voices* authors mention many of these things, as you'll see.

Among places and topics I particularly admire are Staten Island's Noble Maritime Collection where I've explored John Noble's art and the old Sailors Snug Harbor . . . Fort Wadsworth and its handsome Battery Weed beneath the Verrazano . . . Fulton Ferry Brooklyn and its "world's-most-beautiful" Bridge . . . Liberty State Park with its Ellis Island and Liberty Island views . . . the NY Harbor School soon moving mid-harbor to Governors Island . . . and of course South Street Seaport Museum, where I worked at water's edge for sixteen years. And, from which I embarked on so many adventures for the Museum's *South Street Reporter* and *Seaport* magazine. When the Coast Guard helicoptered me out to Ambrose Tower years ago, for instance, the scowl on an officer's face there told me a woman was not welcome. But by day's end he and I were friends and he helped me greatly with my article "Keeping the Light to New York Harbor" (page 76). And the day that ship historian Norman Brouwer and I climbed all around the huge old wooden hulks of sailing ships in Port Johnston, off Staten Island, remains a treasure of a time (see "Port Johnston on a Wintry Harbor Day," page 120). There are so many grand adventures!

Today, my list of beloved harbor vessels, people, and places is long and always changing with new discoveries – the yield of Capt. John Doswell's Working Harbor Committee Hidden Harbor Tours; I am proud to serve on this Committee. WHC's members are rich in harbor knowledge and willing to share it. Thank goodness for the Working Harbor Committee, the Metropolitan Waterfront Alliance, and myriad other harbor-minded groups offering exploration, education, and well-informed advocacy. Ferry routes, waterfront parks, Newtown Creek and Harlem River renaissance plans, and priceless occasions – such as the "3 Queens" harbor evening in which the majestic Cunard liners *QM2*, *QE2*, and *Victoria* sailed together – with fireboat sprayings and fireworks on a chill January night – for the last time before *QE2's* retirement . . . or, Labor Day Sunday's Great North River Tugboat Race & Competition churning down the Hudson – are all seen to by these attentive organizations. Each group has a maritime to-do list of infinite length, from creating new waterfront access to saving historic graving docks to declaring the need for cleats and bollards along public piers. The harbor is fortunate to be in their hands, to be beneficiary to their diverse interpretations and actions.

The *Harbor Voices* anthology also includes reports by several authors who have put their individual New York harbor experiences across in memorable words. Among these are several who wrote well before our time – Melville, Millay, and Whitman among them – because their words are as fresh and true today as the moment they entered a writer's heart and ended up on paper, for handing down to us today.

– Terry Walton, Fall 2008

Harbor Views

The *Harbor Voices* anthology is one person's journey, an intermixing of discoveries written about or read in recent memory (1970s and thereafter) and much newer ones (through summer-fall 2008). This collection conveys my own delight in our harbor over all these years, and in this "Harbor Views" section come some favorite outcomes of these adventurings – the Old Salts remembering things down at South Street and Norman Brouwer's remarks on Hell Gate's treacheries are among them. And Melville's "Circumambulate the City of a dreamy Sabbath afternoon" has always been evocative for me: you can just see the forests of sailing ship masts that he describes. ★ Newer in my life have been five never-a-dull-moment years with the Working Harbor Committee, whose members are encyclopedically savvy about the harbor. Among our several projects is Working Harbor Day, Year 1 of which drew ten fervent participants in downpour and gale; within two years there were thousands. And the harbor waters themselves – written about by long-time environmentalist friend John Mylod and by author John Waldman (I met him at a Long Island book-signing) – remain for me mysterious and powerful. *TW*

Op Sail '76 at South Street Seaport Museum, with familiar visitor Danish square-rigger Danmark *just astern of the Seaport's* Wavertree *and* Peking.

"New York is a city built from the sea . . ."

*W*e live round a sea like frogs round a pond," said Plato, thinking of the Greeks and their Mediterranean. To begin to understand New York, one must really wrap one's mind round that notion. ★ New York is a city built from the sea. Its most vital lines of communication, through all its growth, ran overseas, to other cities that also look outward: Antwerp, Liverpool, Charleston, San Francisco. That heritage is in us now. Our people are here now, coming as they did over the seas, or later by rail or plane, because of the way the city took shape, the way it grew from the half-tide strip on the East River. People voyaged from other places to be here, to build new lives here, to build and rebuild a city from beginnings on that muddy strip to which we are now returning in our time.*

– Peter Stanford, South Street Reporter 1973, South Street Seaport Museum

Old Salts Reminisce
At Seaport Seminar

On December 5, a frosty evening whose chill was hardly cut by the lone gas radiator in 203 Front Street, South Street was proud to be host to a remarkable group of seafaring men in an outstanding meeting in the seminar series.

Speakers were Archie Horka, retired U.S. Lines Captain, who in his early days chased the vanishing breed of vessels carrying mast and sail on our waterfront with the same fervor with which others of his calling chased "skirts"; Fred Harvey, who ran away to sea on a square-rigged whaler, the *Alice Knowles,* in 1900 at age fourteen, and who served as boatswain under Capt. Murphy aboard the immortal *Shenandoah;* Oswald Brett, noted marine artist who has contributed paintings and drawings of *Wavertree* to the forthcoming book on that ship, drawings of the schooners *Caviare* and *America,* and a campaigner for South Street whose letters to the New York *Times,* Alan Villiers and others, have brought new strength to the cause of old ships in our city; Stanley Gerr, who took up sailing in coasting schooners and graduated to serve under Capt. Barker aboard *Tusitala,* New York's last square-rigger, and Robert Herbert, who can name blocks no one else has heard of and who draws up elegant sailing diagrams for our Explorer Scout unit.

The yarns started with bad weather at sea and went on from there. Archie Horka spoke of running half-submerged with full decks in the Roaring Forties and wondering if the ship would ever rise again. Fred Harvey mentioned looking down from the long boat to see whales swimming beneath him. "Please don't come up here," he whispered. He also told the tragic tale of a shipmate who was flipped off a yard and whose bones he had to dig out of the deck. Stanley Gerr promptly related being in the chain locker of a coasting schooner off City Island when the anchor ran away and he danced a death minuet with the flailing links; when he climbed out of the trap the men on deck said, "We were watching for pieces of you coming up the pipe."

Os Brett and Bob Herbert never had a chance to tell their tales as there was much to discuss in these stories. Fred Harvey also related how he earned just one dollar in his first eleven months a-whaling. But, as Archie Horka said, hard and inhuman as the service was in square-rig, it drew men to it, real men.

– Peter Stanford, South Street Reporter 1969, South Street Seaport Museum

Ship Captains & Charitable Works Since 1770 –
The Marine Society of the City of New York

*Marine Society
history, 1995.*

Some time between the Dutch settlement of New Amsterdam and the founding of the American Republic, New York became a major port. Sails filled the lower harbor and pioneered the development that would turn New York into the center of world commerce and communications that it is today.

New York sea captains have written illustrious chapters in this continuing saga of a city built from the sea. And in 1770, when New York was still a British colony, these hard-driving shipmasters formed their own organization, the Marine Society of the City of New York, to express their professional interest, including the diffusion of maritime knowledge and the care of families of shipmasters lost at sea.

Today the immense international commerce of the Port of New York flows through large container ports like Port Elizabeth, built on a marshy backwater of the New Jersey shore at the spot where a band of Marine Society captains sent in a large elegant rowboat to pick up George Washington for his inauguration as the first president of the United States in 1789. Inhabitants and commuting workers in [today's] central city see nothing of this gigantic enterprise – but it is there, and the city's economic sustenance depends upon its operations. . . .

Something of the city's defining character – one could say, its soul – is in the ideas and actions of these sea captains through tumultuous decades, stretching now into centuries, of their dedicated work together. And today, working with the National Maritime Historical Society, which properly regards past, present and future not as separate scenes, but as one living continuum, the Marine Society is increasingly finding its mission in reaching out to carry that maritime story, a story of American character and achievement, to wider circles of Americans.

– *From Walter Cronkite's foreword to* The Marine Society of the City of New York
(1995, by Gerald Barry), on the 225th Anniversary of the Society's founding

NOTE – The Marine Society's founding mission – with George Washington among earliest members – is "to improve maritime knowledge and provide relief to indigent and distressed ship masters, their widows and orphans." The Society's current scholarship program, which "encourages our youth to seek careers in the Maritime Industry," is an extension of that long-standing commitment.

Hudson, Harbor, & the Sea –
Underwater Connections

Atlantic Ocean tides reach more than one hundred fifty miles up the valley and tickle the federal dam at Troy that marks the northern boundary of the estuary portion of the Hudson. Here, too, the waters of the Mohawk River and the upper Hudson watershed meet the estuary and flow seaward toward New York harbor.

Halfway in from the sea, at Poughkeepsie, Bud Tschudin and I operate the M/T Net Co. and fish commercially for shad, herring and blue crab. Although seventy-five miles inland, we rely on the intermixing of fresh and sea waters to support an incredibly diverse and rich abundance of aquatic life in the Hudson.

In fact, the physical and chemical characteristics of estuaries make these special places vital to the health of coastal zones. In the Hudson, they supply the habitats and water quality conditions for the spawning and nursery needs of more than two hundred species of fish: stay-at-home species, such as large-mouth bass, as well as ocean fish like shad, herring, striped bass and sturgeon which move upriver into fresh water each spring to spawn.

Cued by longer days and water temperature, these adult ocean fish come through the harbor on the way to the freshwater areas of their birth, and then return to the sea after spawning. In turn, the young-of-the-year fingerlings feed and grow as they begin their precarious journey back to the sea, and by fall are in the harbor and near-shore coastal waters.

If the young-of-the-year are lucky enough to avoid predator fish and power plant water withdrawals they are supplied with a nutrient-rich "soup" of plankton and other foodstuffs as they descend the river and slowly become acclimated to ocean water. Fresh water from the land rides over the top of heavier sea water and the friction creates an area of suspended plant and animal plankton along with turbid water quality – providing both food and protection for billions of young fish spawned each year in the estuary.

Tidal cycles eventually carry these tiny fish downriver and, along the way, shallow bays, wetlands, submerged aquatic vegetation and the harbor's inter-pier areas provide food, shelter from predators and areas of refuge from the churning tides as well as places for overwintering.

For tiny blue crabs entering the estuary, the harbor is their first refuge. Later, it is also the last stop on an adult female crab's trek downriver before she goes to sea to spawn –

Born in salt-rich waters near the mouth of the Hudson, blue crabs enter the harbor by happenstance, on wind-driven currents, before eventually moving upriver as they molt and grow. They start out as specks in the water and grow to be about the size of an adult man's outstretched hand. On her eighteenth or nineteenth and last molt, a female and male blue crab will mate – unlike most fish which broadcast eggs and sperm into the water and hope for the best. After mating in brackish water, the adult male crab will move upriver into fresh water and the female will move back downriver into the higher salinity waters of the harbor before moving offshore in the spring to spawn.

And like the tidal flow of the Hudson itself, these cycles of life have been repeated for thousands of years, as each year the snow-melt and rainfall from the upriver watershed mix with the flood-thrust from the sea, and provide the building blocks of a critical aquatic ecosystem which is both profound and magical. – *John Mylod*

CHRIS BOWSER

John Mylod, hauling in Hudson River shad.

-- ★ --

Our Harbor Waters – Where Do They Come From & Where Do They Go?

The heart of the harbor is the Upper and Lower New York Bays: auricle and ventricle. The Upper Bay receives the runoff of much of New York State via the Hudson River, saline in summer almost to Poughkeepsie and tidal at all times to Troy. . . . Waters originating from Catskill Mountain bogs, dairy farms of the Mohawk River Valley, little corners of Connecticut,

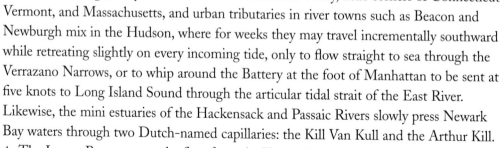

Vermont, and Massachusetts, and urban tributaries in river towns such as Beacon and Newburgh mix in the Hudson, where for weeks they may travel incrementally southward while retreating slightly on every incoming tide, only to flow straight to sea through the Verrazano Narrows, or to whip around the Battery at the foot of Manhattan to be sent at five knots to Long Island Sound through the articular tidal strait of the East River. Likewise, the mini estuaries of the Hackensack and Passaic Rivers slowly press Newark Bay waters through two Dutch-named capillaries: the Kill Van Kull and the Arthur Kill.

★ The Lower Bay connects the flow from the Upper Bay with the near-ocean watershed of the New York Bight, the triangle of submerged shelf and canyon running from Montauk, New York, to Cape May, New Jersey. – *John Waldman, from* Heartbeats in the Muck *(Lyons Press, 1999), which delves into today's environmental situations and active new organizations, and ends with a message not yet of completion but definitely of hope.*

The Port of New York was the busiest in North America throughout the 19th century and the first half of the 20th. It was the busiest in the world for six straight decades, from around 1912 to 1972, and is still among our country's three or four busiest. Its geology takes deserved credit for this early-on prominence. ★ The three waterways that make

Manhattan an island are rivers in name only. In geologic terms the lower Hudson is a fjord. The East River is a tidal strait linking two arms of the sea, New York Bay and Long Island Sound. The Harlem River is a ship canal that, before human intervention, was an impassable collection of creeks and swamps. ★ The greatest natural hazard to shipping in New York harbor was Hell Gate, a curving narrows of the East River lying between the present boroughs of Queens and the Bronx. During the Revolution the British warship H.M.S. *Hussar* struck a reef here and sank, allegedly carrying silver to pay the army, and American prisoners of war. Following the Civil War the reefs were blasted out of Hell Gate in the largest man-made explosions up to that time, detonated by the new wonder of the age, electricity. ★ Today, Hell Gate currents can reach a racing 6-8 knots with powerful eddies and tidal rips. Its slack tide minutes, during which water direction changes fast from upriver to down or back again – are much in the minds of boatmen attempting passage. ★ The harbor's waters rise and fall in a twice-daily tidal range of four to five feet. When high tide, storm, and wind direction coincided in 2002, a restaurant just inland on Beekman Street near the Brooklyn Bridge flooded to table height. ★ Several New York harbor waterway-spanning bridges were the longest of their type in the world when completed – including the suspension spans of the Brooklyn Bridge (1883), George Washington Bridge (1931), and Verrazano-Narrows Bridge (1964). The Bayonne Bridge (1931) between Staten Island and New Jersey was the longest arched bridge in the world, beating the more familiar Sydney Harbor Bridge in Australia by a few feet. – *Norman Brouwer*

"Circumambulate the City . . ."

There now is your insular city of the Manhattoes, belted round by wharves as Indian isles by coral reefs – commerce surrounds it with her surf. Right and left, the streets take you waterward. Its extreme downtown is the battery, where that noble mole is washed by waves, and cooled by breezes, which a few hours previous were out of sight of land. Look at the crowds of water-gazers there.

Circumambulate the city of a dreamy Sabbath afternoon. Go from Corlears Hook to Coenties Slip, and from thence, by Whitehall, northward. What do you see? – Posted like silent sentinels all around the town, stand thousands upon thousands of mortal men fixed in ocean reveries. Some leaning against the spiles; some seated upon the pier-heads; some looking over the bulwarks of ships from China; some high aloft in the rigging, as if striving to get a still better seaward peep. But these are all landsmen; of week days pent up in lath and plaster – tied to counters, nailed to benches, clinched to desks. How then is this! Are the green fields gone? What do they here?

But look! here come more crowds, pacing straight for the water, and seemingly bound for a dive. Strange! Nothing will content them but the extremest limit of the land; loitering under the shady lee of yonder warehouses will not suffice. No. They must get just as nigh the water as they possibly can without falling in. And there they stand – miles of them – leagues. Inlanders all, they come from lanes and alleys, streets and avenues—north, east, south, and west. Yet here they all unite. Tell me, does the magnetic virtue of the needles of the compasses of all those ships attract them thither? – *Herman Melville from "Loomings," the first chapter of* Moby Dick, *1851*

Brooklyn and Manhattan bridges from Pier 16, 1970s.

TERRY WALTON

People – Harbor Jobs & Waterfront Explorations

JOHN SENZER

Tugs? They have owners and skippers and crews. Incoming ships? Pilots guide them in and stevedores and crane crews and straddle-carrier operators unload them. The merchant marine academies at Kings Point and Fort Schuyler? Their graduates operate many of the vessels that do this exacting harbor work, and in turn ships' officers are among the professors who teach them their seamanship skills. All over the harbor, as the Working Harbor Committee's *HarborGuide* set forth in one of its early issues, unseen hands do oftentimes unknown tasks that make the harbor work. From harbor pilot Bill Sherwood and salvage diver Bob Davidson . . . to tanker captain and now professor Capt. Cynthia Robson . . . to Sandy Hook pilot Capt. Tim Ferrie and Port Captain Steven Bendo . . . to the nothing-surprises-them crew of the drift collector *Gelberman* (see page 72) – the Harbor-Jobs people have an awesome list of skills. Capt. Brian McAllister, the late maritime artist Frank Braynard, and Bill Baker of Channel 13 are names we know – they've helped run the harbor or they appreciate it out their office windows, as does Baker. But names known or unknown, harbor people do the work and the rest of us reap the benefits. Or, do the exploring, like the mother – in "We'd Just Pick Up and Go" – who took her two sons on harbor trips to teach them important things. *TW*

The Jobs That Make the Harbor Work . . .
Meet the People Behind the Scenes

Tug captain . . . ferry owner . . . stevedore . . . drawbridge operator . . . Sandy Hook pilot . . . coastal tanker captain – they're all longtime and vital parts of our harbor as city grew from sea, from the 1600s to today. This twelve-person feature, drawn in part from the Working Harbor Committee's *HarborGuide '04,* celebrates the men and women who work where you'll rarely see them – moving vessels, carrying passengers and freight, diving for salvage, recording the waterfront in art and archives – there's no end to the things they do. Our harbor is alive and well, with a renaissance of interest in shorelines, parks, ferries, books – all the yield of the river, strait, and lower harbor waterways that interconnect our myriad parts.

Pamela Hepburn,
Tugboat Captain & Preservationist

★ **Occupation:** Tug Pegasus Preservation Project Director; preservationist; licensed tugboat captain with 500-ton Master's License

★ **Vessel/place:** Tugboat *Pegasus* of the Tug Pegasus Preservation Project, a museum chartered by NY State

★ **Harbor location:** Morris Canal Basin

★ **Number of harbor years:** 32

★ **Typical day's work:** "No way is there a typical day at work. There are office days and meeting days and tug days. Days in my pajamas, days when I have to look somewhat reasonable, and days when I have to get really dirty. I coordinate everything to do with maintenance and restoration of a 97-year-old tugboat, according to American Bureau of Shipping standards, as well as write grants and coordinate volunteers. • We're entering the third year of the Police Athletic League's Maritime Adventure Program – one of many programs envisioned to bring people to the water and their city's history. It's the most fun to see people feel ownership of a waterfront that has been closed off to them for so long."

GORDON MOORE

★ **Highlight:** "My year docking ships for Moran in 1998. The primary function of a tugboat is to do 'ship assist.' Ship assist is a fantastic dynamic of pushing and pulling passenger liners and container ships . . . hours of boredom and seconds of sheer terror. You're dancing with the ship in very close quarters. New York is the only port that docks vessels perpendicular to the stream in all currents, not just in slack water. Tricky!! What a great job. But, I had to retire because living aboard for a week at a time was not compatible with raising my daughter Alice."

★ **Harbor interconnections:** Ran Hepburn Marine Towing for ten years, has support from the tug industry for the Pegasus Project. Serves as trustee for many organizations supporting historic vessels, including the Lighthouse Tender *Lilac* and the North River Historic Ship Society. Also, spends time campaigning for maritime use of waterfront property.

★ **Comment:** Pamela has "always had a passion for old stuff and how it is constructed." Her pleasure is to preserve a piece of history, whether it's a 1953 diesel engine or the mortises in a wheelhouse. Terms like "bulkheads" and "beaded deck beams" roll off her tongue. Of her vision, she says: "My druthers would be to have *Pegasus* underway for 6 to 8 hours a day. Trouncing around on a big, safe, strong vessel is a joyful thing." – *Lee Gruzen*

Pegasus *today is completing substantial needed restoration work, readying her for harbor education programs for youth, and is on the National Register of Historic Places. See page 52.*

★

Glenn W. Hodgdon, Coastal Tanker Captain

★ **Occupation:** Ship captain
★ **Vessel:** *Keystone Texas,* a 685-foot tanker that carries oil from Port Arthur, Texas, to Bayonne, New Jersey, every month, stopping at Charleston and Wilmington.

★ **Harbor location:** Bayonne, NJ
★ **Number of Harbor years:** 27
★ **Typical day's work:** "Most days I'm up by 6 a.m. I go up to the bridge and look at the charts and make sure we're on course. I check our speed, I check weather reports. Then I go through the items we're going to attend to that day – maintenance checks, safety programs like fire and life boat drills, routine inspections on pyrotechnics and cargo gear. Every morning's a different place in the water, and different projects."

★ **Challenging event:** "In 1993 we collided with another ship. We had been at anchor for a day wait-  ing to go into the dock in Galveston. The current was strong. I had a pilot aboard the vessel. I ordered a tug to assist, but the pilot said we didn't need it. The other vessel was a liquefied petro- leum gas ship – and it was getting too close. There came a point when I took over and backed the vessel full. We still ended up hitting the other ship. It was sheer adrenaline rush. No one was hurt – and you can repair steel. There was of course a Coast Guard investigation and all ended well."

★ **Harbor interconnections:** "We're lucky to have Moran shipping. They get Coast Guard clearance and do all our docking arrangements." When navigating the harbor, Keystone Texas uses Interport Pilots.

★ **Comment:** "My first job was on an oil tanker sailing from Staten Island, by way of the Goethals Bridge, to Texas. As a young third mate from Maine, I found New York harbor a real eye opener. • It's been a great career. But I have to give my wife a lot of credit. It's demanding on anybody's marriage." • Capt. Hodgdon will retire in a couple of years. "I'd like to get into investigation of accidents, maybe a position with the National Transportation Safety Board." He is concerned about the future of the industry: "The American merchant marine is disappearing because of foreign competition. We can't compete with third world countries in shipbuilding and in hiring crews. I hope people can be made aware that the merchant marine plays a big role in the way this country runs." – *Alison Simko, 2004*

★

Bill Sherwood,
Sandy Hook Pilot

★ **Occupation:** Captain, President of NY Sandy Hook Pilots Association

★ **Harbor location:** Staten Island

★ **Number of harbor years:** 32

★ **Typical day's work:** "I respond to letters, peruse the *Journal of Commerce* and *Lloyd's Shipping Register*, and field two to three dozen phone calls on ships arriving and leaving, draft, tonnage, size, where vessels are to be docked, and other matters. I speak to regulatory agencies regarding inspection procedures. I'm the point of contact for the Coast Guard and the State Board of Pilot Commissioners to disseminate information to the pilots."

★ **Challenging event:** "The destruction of the World Trade Center. The participation of the Sandy Hook pilots is and was extraordinarily inspiring to me. We had every piece of equipment we owned at the Battery wall. I was handling the show on this end. After evacuating thousands of people, pilots refueled fire engines from pilot boat fuel stocks, and delivered food and water."

★ **Harbor interconnections:** Besides coordinating with NY and NJ police harbor units, Coast Guard, and Port Authority, Capt. Sherwood works with the Army Corps of Engineers (responsible for dredging), and with NOAA (National Oceanic and Atmospheric Administration). "We have found it convenient to be close to NOAA. They do all the soundings, the bottom profiles of the harbor – and they're greatly under-funded. We offer them a place to tie up, some hospitality, and in exchange, they sound places our pilots are suspect of."

★ **Comment:** As they approach New York harbor, foreign ships or U.S. ships coming from a foreign port are boarded by a Sandy Hook pilot about 20 miles from the Verrazano-Narrows Bridge for guidance through the heavy commercial and recreational traffic that moves in the harbor's narrow, turbulent channels. The pilots' knowledge of water depths, shoals and reefs, anchorages, cables and pipelines, tides, and weather is unsurpassed, honed by years of training. • Experienced in handling all types of vessels, a pilot may find himself guiding a cruise ship outbound, pausing at the pilot house, and boarding an inbound petroleum tanker. • "Our 82 pilots cover a fairly large range, from Atlantic City to Albany, and from Sandy Hook to Point Judith, Rhode Island." The pilots make 12,000 trips a year, guiding traffic that generates more than $12 billion in annual economic activity. – *Alison Simko, 2004*

★

Naima Rauam, NY Harbor Artist

★ **Occupation**: Artist
★ **Place**: Fulton Fish Market and NY harbor
★ **Harbor location**: Has been painting tugs, fishing boats, and harbor construction projects for longer than her appearance would suggest, and has

also found time to become a pilot and aviation artist (two paintings in Smithsonian's Air and Space Museum), race car driver (she paints them, too), and the more or less official artist-in-residence at the Fulton Fish Market, where she began painting in the 1960s. She double-dips, too, combining helicopter lessons with aerial photography for her two-year task of documenting in watercolor the building of the new Cross Bay Bridge – her work an epic project now in the Smithsonian Institution collection.

★ **Typical day's work**: "I get up in the middle of the night, hop on my bicycle and pedal down to the Fulton Fish Market. Instantly energized by the frenetic activity of the Market, I grab my sketch book and camera and start recording details of scenes depicting the 180-year-old business of selling seafood in lower Manhattan. Then I go to my studio (happily, in the middle of the Market) and start crafting these notes into watercolors."

★ **Highlight/challenging event**: "I did finished watercolors on location until that fateful night with the halibut. It was 3 a.m. at the Fulton Fish Market. There I was, paint box situated on an empty fish crate, a cup of water on the ground, paper balanced on my knee, brushes in hand, capturing the details of a wonderful halibut in a box with its tail flopping over the side. Suddenly a journeyman hauled away this magnificent fish I was painting. It had been sold and had to be delivered! I hastily committed final details to memory as the flopping fish tail bounced away down the street. • Once while prowling around Caddell's yard on Staten Island, gathering sketches and photos, I encountered a barge resting in a dry dock being repaired. I peeped under it and saw a welder. I crawled in to take a closer look and witnessed a splendid scene of the welder's arc sparkling in the darkness under the great flat expanse of the barge."

★ **Comment:** "The Fish Market is a great link to New York harbor, one of the last remnants of the city's real working waterfront. Since I've been painting at the Market, I have become aware of the waters beyond it. When daylight chases away the fishmongers, I look to other aspects of the waterfront for inspiration." – *Jack Putnam*

Naima adds this in 2008 – "In 2005 the Fulton Fish Market left South Street for a new home in the Bronx. While I frequently visit and still paint Market scenes, the waterfront now commands more of my attention and I look fondly upon the many interesting vessels and marvelous bridges gracing our waterways. There is much inspiration here."

Steven P. Kalil, Shipyard Executive

★ **Occupation:** President, Caddell Dry Dock and Repair Co., Inc.

★ **Place:** Staten Island

★ **Harbor location:** On the Kill Van Kull, foot of Broadway

★ **Number of harbor years:** 30

★ **Typical day's work:** "Every day presents a new challenge. Whether it's coming to an agreement with a customer or addressing government regulations, no two days are alike. I spend much of my time conferring with the dock master, machinists, carpenters, and iron-workers. While I'm in the office most of the time, I like being in the yard and on the dry docks." • Steve is familiar with the hands-on work that takes place on a dry dock. He began his career at Caddell's as a carpenter in 1975, and later learned to manage the yard and its day-to-day operations. He became president in 1989.

JEAN PREECE

★ **Highlight:** "We put the historic Portuguese bark the *Gazela* of Philadelphia on dry dock #4 so her volunteer crew could make repairs. The replica of Henry Hudson's *Half Moon* has been here twice, and we have worked on three of South Street Seaport Museum's historic ships – the *Ambrose* and the tall ships *Peking* and *Wavertree*." • Steve's support of historic vessels and non-profit ships comes from his interest in the preservation of maritime history, and reflects the sensibilities of shipyard owner John B. Caddell II and the Caddell family.

★ **Harbor interconnections:** "At Caddell we service the waterfront – barges, tugs, tankers, and ferries. I work closely with many ship owners, and we have relationships going back for years."

★ **Comment:** One of Steve's special connections is with the Noble Maritime Collection, where he has been a long-time member of the board of trustees and is chairman emeritus. During the 1990s he was part of the Noble Crew, a group of volunteers who rehabilitated the building that houses the museum.

Over the nine years it took to make the building habitable, he spent many weekend days using his skill as a carpenter, recalling his early days at the Caddell shipyard, to restore this landmark.
– *Julie Laudicina, 2004*

★

Norman J. Brouwer, Maritime Historian

★ **Occupation**: Maritime historian and author
★ **Place**: Home office in Bayside, Queens
★ **Harbor locations**: Libraries at Fort Schuyler, Bronx; Kings Point, Long Island; buoy tender *Lilac*, Hudson River/Pier 40
★ **Number of harbor years**: 36 + 9 as merchant seaman
★ **Typical day's work**: "There is no typical day at work! I bury myself in archival materials about the history of the Port of New York, and am currently writing histories and biographies for the Merchant Marine Hall of Fame at Kings Point, and doing ship histories for the U.S. Maritime Administration. • This harbor is a strategic location – I've done research all over the world and researchers from all over the world pass through New York. • I also track ships as the editor of the *International Register of Historic Ships*, and answer questions when people send them. I use the Internet more and more for research and communication. • It's a fine job –

I pursue my hobby and get paid for it."
★ **Highlight**: "My first trip to the Falkland Islands [South Atlantic] surviving American sailing ships survey project in 1976 – landing in the middle of the world's largest outdoor museum of wooden sailing ships. It's a place that time forgot. Port Stanley had air service – one flight a week, steamship service had ended, people were living in isolated conditions as if still in the 1930s. All around was the odor of burning peat heating the homes and pubs – kind of a primeval gloom until the sun came out."
★ **Harbor interconnections**: Wrote 100+ articles for South Street Seaport Museum's *Seaport* magazine, and spent many years as SSSM curator and acting librarian while maintaining the Museum's extensive photo archive. Still gathering research for a completed draft of the 1860-2008 companion volume to Albion's *The Rise of New York Port, 1815-1860*. Serves on boards of Tug Pegasus Preservation Project, Lighthouse Tender Lilac; member Steamship Historical Society, Working Harbor Committee.
★ **Comment**: I worked with Norman for years and cannot count the times he has said, in answer to my harbor history question, "I don't know about that, really, except for . . ." and then coming up with intriguing facts that are precisely what I wanted. • Of NY harbor he says: "People should see Brando's movie 'On the Waterfront' – then look today and see how much activity is still here – in tonnage, NY is still the busiest seaport in the Eastern U.S. – *Terry Walton*

★

NY City
Drawbridge Operator

★ **Occupation:** Drawbridge operator

★ **Place:** Any one of 25 movable bridges in New York City

★ **Number of harbor years:** 17

★ **Typical day's work:** "Our workday consists of inspections and, of course, bridge openings. Each shift is eight hours. While all bridges have a control house, not all bridges are manned. Some operators stay at one bridge for their entire shift, while others are based at a central location and travel to various bridges in DOT trucks. Requests for bridge openings are either phoned in to the DOT office, or a ship can contact a manned bridge via radio."

★ **Highlight:** "Obviously we see the most activity when a bridge must be opened. One operator remains in the control house, and a second oversees safety gates and lights. Some gates are automatic while others must be set in place manually. When vehicular traffic is safely stopped, the bridge is

BERNARD ENTE

opened. Sometimes it's difficult to convince traffic to stop! Nobody wants to wait for a bridge to open. • As soon as the marine traffic is clear, the bridge is closed.

A quick inspection to make sure everything is in proper alignment, and the safety gates are removed.

The entire process usually takes ten minutes. Most motorists are polite, but we can be the targets of nasty remarks, oftentimes unprintable!"

★ **Harbor interconnections:** Regulated by U.S. Coast Guard.

★ **Comment:** Quoting the DOT's web page, "Operating under various federal mandates that require 24 hour per day, 7 day per week coverage at many facilities, the principal requirement of this group is to provide safe and expeditious passage for all marine and vehicular traffic under and on the movable bridges." – *Bernard Ente, 2004*

★

Bob Davidson,
a.k.a. Bob the Diver

★ **Occupation:** "Underwater Artisan" – at least that's what the insurance company says; does salvage and recovery, and wheel and shaft work

★ **Places:** Waterways throughout NY, NJ, Connecticut, Massachusetts, Pennsylvania

★ **Harbor location:** As above

★ **Number of harbor years:** 20

★ **Typical day's work:** For Davidson there is no typical day. "I do everything. I do propeller changes, I do shaft changes, I do any type of underwater maintenance. I do salvage. • The neat thing about my job is I don't think there's a day when I can go in the water and say I know everything. And I'll never – if I live to be a thousand, I'll never know everything. But you know what? I can learn. The biggest key to my job is common sense. • The average person tries to reinvent the wheel when

they do a job. They over-think it. My theory is, keep it simple as possible. I'm probably the laziest man on the face of the earth. I work a lot of hours, but I try and do it simple. If I can do the thing in a single lift, we'll do a single lift. We won't rig it to this, to that, you know, make a nightmare out of it."

★ **Challenging event:** "There's been a lot! I usually get the jobs no one else wants to get involved with. I've worked heavy construction jobs. Done heavy salvage work, and large propellers. • The thing is, everybody's trying to do things cheap. It does make it harder. There are lots of jobs where if we just had one good crane and one good pump we could raise a boat in an hour or two. It's all the more time-consuming and hard on my old body."

★ **Harbor interconnections:** With a reputation for being creative, fast, and resourceful, Bob is notorious for making tough jobs seem easy. When a boat sinks, a prop snags, or a rudder gets lost, local mariners reach for Bob's holographic blue business card. He works on all manner of vessel from ferries and fishing boats to tugs and motor yachts. He also assists dock-builders and shipyards. His specialty – using explosives to loosen larger propellers.

★ **Comment:** Known for saying, "We do it Bob's way or Bob goes home. Simple as that." – *Jessica*

DuLong, 2004 (Jessica DuLong's work has appeared in *Newsweek International*, *Rolling Stone*, *Maritime Reporter and Engineering News*, and other publications. As engineer on retired NYC fireboat *John J. Harvey*, she runs five 600 hp diesels on trips along the Hudson.)

James Devine, Stevedore

★ **Occupation:** President, NY Container Terminal
★ **Place:** NW Shore, Staten Island
★ **Harbor location:** Arthur Kill/Inner Harbor
★ **Number of harbor years:** 34
★ **Typical day's work:** "I coordinate the movement of men and machines to load and discharge cargo efficiently. In the office, I check statistics of previ-

ous days, reviewing efficiency, productivity, deployment of people. I work closely with managers, supervisors, and superintendents, and I learn a lot by walking around, observing minute-to-minute business, managing my best by walking around or driving around, talking with the laborers themselves. Some go to their offices, do planning from the conference room, but I like to see the day-to-day activities, go out to where the action is."

★ **Challenging event:** "My challenge right now is to plan for the future, work with the Port of New York on further expansion, the need for lots of man hours, new berths for the ever increasing volume of containership cargo coming into the harbor."

★ **Harbor Interconnections:** "We work with the Port Authority, the Army Corps of Engineers, the trucking community to make sure that we have a good relationship with them, that we meet their needs. Same with rail carriers, we work with them to coordinate the movement of trains. We work with U.S. Customs and the Coast Guard on safety issues – we have a good and steady interface with them."

★ **Comment:** "In 1956, we had 33,000 longshoremen; they created the character of the waterfront. But in 2006 there are fewer than 4,000 longshoremen despite the hundred-fold increase in tonnage moving into and out of the port. We have significantly improved cargo-handling efficiency, to the point were it's virtually invisible. Last year there were 4,000 container vessels in the port and they handled millions of tons of cargo. In 1956 there were 12,000 ships moving substantially less cargo. The challenge is, with the ever-increasing demand for imported goods, we have effectively used up the capacity footprint of these terminals, in the Port of New York and New Jersey, so how do we move forward to continue to accommodate growth? We're working to maximize the efficiency of our capacity by creating more upland area. We're at 24/7 and the goods materialize." – *Terry Walton*

Capt. Cynthia Robson, Professor, Nautical Science

★ **Occupation:** As professor of Nautical Science at United States Merchant Marine Academy, Kings Point, teach basic seamanship through advanced ship handling and navigation

★ **Vessel/place:** Most recent command: tanker *Ex-Exxon Jamestown*

★ **Harbor location:** USMMA, Kings Point, NY

★ **Number of harbor years:** 13

★ **Typical day's work:** "Teaching at USMMA, I spend class time with midshipmen, as well as laboratory time using full mission or part task simulators – for practical application of shiphandling theory. The full mission simulator creates a virtual reality of a ship's bridge wherein midshipmen can execute many passages, including NY harbor: from pilot boarding at Ambrose light, navigating the Verrazano Narrows channel, anchoring at Stapleton, meeting vessels in Kill Van Kull, to docking in Port Elizabeth. The part-task simulator permits up to 24 midshipmen to handle their own vessels and interact simultaneously. I've developed scenarios in which they transit narrow channels, dock, undock, anchor, rescue a man overboard given changing weather conditions on vessels in various ports worldwide, including NY."

★ **Challenging moments:** "When I was Master of the *Jamestown*, we had a distress call from four men on a sailboat that had lost her mainsail in a South Pacific storm, and we had to come to their rescue. I maneuvered the *Jamestown* next to the sailboat and checked safety of crew and the condition of their vessel. We sent a fuel line plus needed food, water, and dry clothes, and they were able to head to

shore. No, I wasn't nervous, just focused on the lives to be saved. • There are other kinds of challenges for me as a female aboard ship. Once as chief mate, when I was headed back to my ship in Corpus Christi, the security guard would not let me enter the port to go to the ship. 'The only women on the docks are the wrong kind of women,' he stated. I had to call the Port Captain before I was allowed to return to my vessel. Another time, headed to the *Jamestown* to take command for the first time, I joined several crew members late at night in a launch to the ship out at anchor. One asked me which ship I was going to. When I stated the *Jamestown*, he replied, "I sure hope you can cook - the last one was no good at all." The crew and I had a good laugh as they signed articles the next morning. • I remember NY harbor right after 9/11. I was teaching ship-handling at USMMA using an ex Coast Guard harbor tug, and a CG fireboat. We were called to serve helping the NY fire department. The whole harbor was closed; we carried supplies (everything from McDonald's fries to equipment and clothes) and personnel. It was eerie, to be on NY harbor, zooming across it in one of our boats: it was totally

empty, totally closed, glass calm. I remember the oddest sight - all along the Battery Park walkway were baby carriages sitting there, very expensive prams, just left there as people fled; the carriages stayed there for weeks in silent testimony."

★ **Harbor interconnections:** "It was a goal of mine, to be part of the Marine Society of the City of New York. As a master mariner I was attracted to them in support of their twofold mission: originally to take care of the widows and orphans of seaman lost at sea, and ship captains in need; and today, to help with maritime scholarships and education including support for the two local maritime academies (USMMA and NY Maritime), and the NY Harbor School. When I applied, I was told I was the first woman to join and that they were so honored to have me apply. Now I am honored to serve as an officer on the Standing Committee of this fine organization. • Today in my work at USMMA, we work with the Sandy Hook Pilots, who donate their time and expertise to our Pilot Aboard scenario for realism. I also serve on the USCG Navigation Safety Advisory Council, which advises the USCG in many aspects, including navigation aids and rules of the road."

★ **Comment:** "I love my job. When I was sailing as master of *Jamestown*, taking her through the Panama Canal, a reporter asked my goals for the future. 'I really want to teach at Kings Point,' I answered. Well, someone overheard and called me and offered me the job. I love being a part of the education of future marine officers. I love it when they come back and tell me about their jobs, once teenagers and now mature contributors as ship officers and shore-side executives." – *Terry Walton*

Sabato "Sal" Catucci, Stevedore CEO

★ **Occupation:** CEO, American Stevedoring, Inc.
★ **Vessel/place:** Red Hook Marine Terminal, Brooklyn; March Street Terminal, Port Newark
★ **Harbor location:** as above
★ **Number of harbor years:** 48
★ **Typical day's work:** For some time until spring 2008, Sabato Catucci was in crisis mode*. He had built a thriving business handling cargo containers, lumber, coffee, and cacao beans, but the Port

Authority of New York and New Jersey told him it would not extend his lease of Piers 6-12. The lease issue occupied most of his waking hours. • "I make telephone calls to politicians and people that want to help. . . . We're here to resolve the issues and negotiate. . . . The only reason I need a lease is to keep my customers happy. They know I'm not giving up," he'd declare.

★ **Highlight/challenging event:** Not surprisingly, Catucci highlights this lease issue as the most challenging event in his work thus far. "People say I fight with everybody. I fight with everybody only

because I fight for what I believe in. If you're not willing to fight for what you believe in you just fold and go under. . . . As long as I'm alive we'll be here."

★ **Harbor interconnections:** Catucci grew up working on the waterfront. At 18, he drove a truck for his father and at 25 started his own trucking company servicing the Port of New York. "I liked the waterfront because it was something different every day." • In 1993, American Stevedoring (ASI) took over operations of Red Hook Marine Terminal in Brooklyn under lease from the Port of New York and New Jersey. Red Hook's container volume reached an all-time high of over 120,000 containers and 45,000 tons of break-bulk cargo, as well as 422,000 tons of bulk cargo. • At Port Newark, ASI operates a 20-acre container/barge handling facility that provides direct access to the nationwide rail and highway network, as well as a 14-acre warehouse and CFS service. Linked by cross-harbor barge, the Elizabeth facility allows shippers to receive or deliver cargo in either Brooklyn or Newark.

★ **Comment:** Sal Catucci received the Working Harbor Committee's first Distinguished Service Award, March 2004, "for bringing fresh vision and high performance to the working Port of New York & New Jersey." – *Jessica DuLong*

* Crisis no longer. After harbor-wide protestations on the importance of American Stevedoring's work in NY harbor, Sal Catucci's lease was renewed through 2017.

★

Steven Bendo,
Vessel Operations
Port Captain, COSCO,
Member ILA Local 1964

★ **Occupation:** As Port Captain for a shipping company, coordinate containership vessel operations and provide stowage planning for terminals to load by

★ **Vessel/place:** Port Elizabeth, NJ

★ **Harbor location:** Port Elizabeth container terminal, beyond Bayonne Bridge in Newark Bay/Elizabeth Channel

★ **Number of harbor years:** 11, including prior service as tug deckhand, ferry captain, chief mate/deep sea

★ **Typical day's work:** "Pick a day! No two are the same and there are always surprises. When we have a vessel coming in, I compile loading information, submit a loading plan for the terminal, contact the terminal to confirm a berth's available, and arrange labor start time. Then I'll arrange boarding times with the Sandy Hook pilots and order tugs for inbound transit. On other days, I'll liaise with various COSCO slot charter partners on loading issues, approve out-of-gauge loading requests, issue coastal schedules for incoming vessels working with other ports such as Boston, Charleston, and Norfolk, so we'll have an outline of vessel calls up or down the coast."

★ **Challenging moments:** "There are all sorts of these! Anything from containership emergencies in

bad weather, or special circumstances such as offloading a large yacht using a floating crane provided by an outside crane company. The challenge is, in dealing with a $5 million yacht, containers

aren't inherently set up for this kind of thing. But everything went smoothly. Also, in a high-wind situation, we can occasionally have a broken mooring line – then I call in the tugs and everything is secured again."

★ **Harbor interconnections:** "We work with the Coast Guard, pilots, tugs, terminal operators, and others on a regular basis."

★ **Comment:** "Since I've been in this job, I've watched the harbor being transformed into the next century with dredging, terminal upgrades, planning services that'll be available in the future. Seeing all this is one of the greatest things I can imagine."

– *Terry Walton*

★ ★ ★

NOTE – Ben Gibberd's handsome book New York Waters *(Globe Pequot Press, 2007) has fine additional working waterfront portraits: eel fisherman, ship propeller repairman, Circle Line guide among them.*

Richard L. Rath ...
A Hero of South Street

TODAY – Dick Rath's work (1972/97) is honored in the missions of SSSM, WHC, NY Harbor School, and other programs for underserved youth.

Dick Rath, longtime trustee of South Street Seaport Museum and National Maritime Historical Society, editor of *Boating* and *Yachting* magazines, coasting skipper, jazz musician and advocate of far-out causes, died on 20 November 1996.

When I first met Rath, on a business trip to Puerto Rico in February 1964, he was skipper of a small inter-island freighter, *M/V Explorer*, which carried (and sometimes towed) odd cargoes to nearby Virgin Islands. A tall, lanky, quizzical-looking man, he had a friendly air occasionally overlaid with a cinematic tough-guy way of talking. I came to call him just "Rath" to mock his use of this monosyllabic city-desk growl in answering his phone. He brought me up to date, I well remember, on a Novy schooner I had spotted in the harbor on prior visits. . . .

I met Rath again in the fall of 1966. He had just taken up work as associate editor of *Boating* magazine. We talked about schooners again. My wife Norma and I owned the 43-foot Alden schooner *Athena* then, and Dick, the charming, wide-hipped, centerboarder *March Heir*, which had belonged to my college classmate Peter Longyear. Rath and I took to having long lunches and memorable evenings, talking about schooners and the embryonic idea of bringing a surviving fishing schooner Norma and I had found into South Street, where there were some fine old waterfront buildings we dreamt of saving.

It turned out he had his own picture of a schooner in the East River – a dream of taking deprived city kids out fishing in a real Gloucesterman, in the old-fashioned way, to find new bearings in their lives. [see *Pioneer's* work in "City Kids Want More," facing page]

When in the spring of 1967 the Museum opened a small office at 16 Fulton Street, in the historic buildings of Schermerhorn Row, Rath saw us shivering over our typewriters in the unheated fish stall, and next day turned up with a gas radiator he had liberated somewhere. He

Rath as Pioneer *captain (in beret) and as city park trombonist.*

City Kids Want More –
Schooner *Pioneer* as All-Hands Teacher

At times the main gaff lay at undignified angles that first morning aboard the schooner *Pioneer* – the brawn hauling on peak and throat halyards was inexperienced brawn, young and tough from New York City streets and unaccustomed to being told "Haul away!" and "Avast!" ★ The boys were on board to learn some sea disciplines and loves that Staten Island ferries and Manhattan sightseeing boats – the sum of their nautical experience – hadn't been able to offer. They had come by subway from Harlem and High Bridge youth centers in South Bronx, recruited by New York City's Youth Services Agency in a program sponsored jointly by YSA and the five-year-old-and-thriving South Street Seaport Museum. . . . ★ No one knew in Seaport or City that first morning just how well the city youths would take to the program newly set up for them – a summer 1971 series of weekend and two-week cruises along the coast to ports like Stonington, Vineyard Haven, and Gloucester. Boys and girls age 13-19, from backgrounds as diverse as anything New York City can offer, were involved. ★ Some came straight from the streets. Others came through the Seaport itself, young volunteers already familiar with Seaport programs and eager for the same sea lessons as their YSA counterparts. ★ The goal of this mixture of city and schooner has been for all the young people to learn of ships and the sea and each other, and for all to be drawn into regular Seaport programs like chantey-singing, seamanship classes, and maintenance work on the several Seaport vessels – specifically the 279-foot square-rigger *Wavertree*, red-hulled *Ambrose* lightship (retired several years ago from her station off Ambrose Channel), and the old 75-foot Gloucester fishing schooner *Caviare*. ★ That *Pioneer* herself was the vessel for the task was known. She's 65 feet long and beamy and stable – an 86-year-old gaff-rigged schooner once working in the Delaware River iron- and steel-beam trade. Lately from Gloucester, Massachusetts, where her owner lovingly rebuilt her and worked her hard until his death, she is now berthed at the Seaport's pier at South and Fulton streets on the East River. That the young people were eager to try the program was known too – 200 signed up immediately for the YSA swimming tests to qualify, enough to fill the program for the whole first summer. – *Terry Walton, from an article in* Sail *Magazine, March 1972*

City youth "learn their lines" aboard Pioneer.

found that Con Ed had not turned off the gas so he hooked up the radiator, a wonderful machine that soon had us toasty warm and feeling much better about life.

He made many people feel better about life, in many ways, always with an eye for old schooners, kids in hopeless situations and underdogs anywhere. In 1970 he took over the iron schooner *Pioneer* in South Street, a landmark step for the fledgling museum. We had inherited her from Russell Grinnell of Gloucester, a great friend of Rath's who was killed in an accident in his waterfront construction business. Rath immediately had the ship out sailing to new horizons with former drug abusers in crew. He attracted the support of the Astor Foundation (which had turned down all prior appeals from the museum) and with this and other help soon established the Pioneer Marine School, taking on young people in trouble, to graduate them into new careers and new lives. Rath's impossible dream yielded real-life results. Among them, the day a Martha's Vineyard boatyard operator called to ask where he could get more of these kids from the streets of New York.

– *Peter Stanford,* Sea History *Magazine, 1997*

NOTE – Incidentally, as an editor with a keen sense of wordsmith humor, Dick Rath named his own harbor vessel – a jaunty ferro-cement lifeboat with an upright deckhouse – Irregardless. *We went one better, amending her name to* Disregardless. *TW*

★ *Changes with time: Today, at age 104,* Pioneer *still sails actively for the Seaport Museum, which recently celebrated the 40th anniversary of its founding. And today as well, city kids from all boroughs participate in the New York Harbor School (see page 146) as well as youth programs by the Working Harbor Committee, Noble Maritime Collection, National Maritime Historical Society and others.*

Three Weeks Became Thirty-Two Years – George Carloss of Sweet's

TODAY – *Sweet's Restaurant (1993) closed for a time in 1991 for restoration, and then, sadly, closed for good.*

George Carloss, born January 5, 1930, Nashville, Tennessee, son of Samuel D. Carloss and Barbara V. Rhea Carloss, is the embodiment of the fine traditions of Sweet's, the famous fish restaurant which stood at the corner of South and Fulton streets for 147 years, and where he served as waiter and sometimes confidant to the rich, famous – and everyone else – for over three decades. George's daughters have graduated from Vassar and Brown and have begun their own careers, and he retired when the landmark eatery closed.

I started working in the hotels in 1942 as a busboy. During the early years of World War Two, I worked every evening after school as well as during the summers. By watching the older employees, especially the waiters, captains, and maitre d's, I became greatly impressed and fascinated with their grace, dignity, charm, and professionalism. I was attentive and diligent, and learned very well. By the year of 1948 I was in the process of becoming a waiter.

MINDA NOVEK

I worked in the Read House in Chattanooga, in the Hotel Peabody in Memphis, in the famous Vanderbilt in Nashville, in the Colonial Williamsburg Inn in Virginia, getting lots of experience, then on to Chicago for the Edgewater Beach Hotel, the Palmer House, and the Blackstone.

By 1950 it was time to serve my country in Korea, which I did, and was very proud in doing so. Returning to the United States, after a very short time of scouting and looking I decided to pursue the same field as before I left, since many fields were not open to minorities during those crucial and trying times. So I went back to doing the thing I knew best, which I could rely on, and that was being a dining room waiter, for which I have no regret.

I got a job at J.P. Morgan Bank, Number 23 Wall Street, and met many great people: General Dwight D. Eisenhower, General Douglas MacArthur, General George C. Marshall, General Omar Bradley, Alfred P. Sloan, Senator John F. Kennedy, Edward R. Murrow, and Fidel Castro, to name a few.

"Sweet's Refectory"

Today, as a century and more before, crisp-creased tablecloths at Sweet's are of heavy cotton, spotlessly white. East River light washes pale and bright through windows on Fulton and South streets. Arched wooden fans with delicate spool-and-spindle turnings trim the tops of the windows, whose brittle old glass is set in deep-molded frames. The bar, dark and polished wood, stands solid in late-last-century opulence, sparkled by its gleaming glass mirror, its corps of richly colored bottles. The warm and ravishing smells of fish and fresh bread fill the clean, plain rooms.

There is always a curious sense of homecoming at Sweet's Restaurant in Schermerhorn Row – people seem to feel its welcome the first time they ever see the place. . . .

*– Ellen Fletcher Rosebrock, Seaport
Magazine 1982, South Street
Seaport Museum
Photographs by Chris Maynard*

★ *Changes with time – Sweet's, once famous as the oldest fish restaurant in the City, closed some years ago.*

Sweet's diners, 1981. Earlier visitors have included Admirals Nimitz and Halsey, sportsmen Casey Stengel and Joe Frazier, entertainers Arthur Godfrey and Lena Horne, and an endless further list of familiar names. Still earlier came ship captains, who, as The New Yorker *wrote some years ago, would "congregate at a big round table, spin yarns, argue, move dishes around the table cloth to illustrate some big hour in the life of an old clipper ship."*

I left the bank after several years to work at a well-known restaurant uptown. There's where I met a fine gentleman by the name of Andrew H. Gerzel, who influenced me to come to work at Sweet's, in 1960, where he was manager and part owner. And I am very, very glad I did.

There's where I met the principal owner and president of the Sweet's organization, Miss Lea Lake, her sister Miss Queenie MacFarland, and Mrs. Billie Gerzel, Mr. G's wife. They were extremely smart, compassionate people. We were all of us – waiters and everyone – a happy family.

I remember wondering about Sweet's at first. "It's so remote. What kind of place is this?" It looked like a building that had seen the turn of many centuries, and I had gotten so used to the glamorous and glittering hotels and nightclubs. But I said, "Yes, this looks like one good place to work. I'll try it out for two or three weeks," and two or three weeks turned out to be thirty-two years, which should tell you something. It was so nice, the years seemed short.

Miss Lake and Mr. G. ran a tight ship. Because of the great demand for tables, no reservations were ever taken in case of lateness or no-shows, and no parties were ever seated unless complete. Our fish was from the Fulton Market down the street, the freshest ever. In the blackout of 1965 Miss Lake and Mr. G. remained open for business, serving the public in their very professional manner by candlelight.

Sweet's customers have always been from all walks of life – the bulls and bears of Wall Street, prominent lawyers and judges, shipping magnates and oil tycoons, tobacco and cocoa importers, trawler captains and fishing merchants, and some of the greatest show personalities of our time, Buddy Hackett, Don Rickles, Lucille Ball, Burt Lancaster, Lena Horne – and on to just ordinary people.

Today there are no more trawlers, no more shrimp boats, no more sea captains. Where did they all go? When Miss Lake left on a Friday four years ago I had no idea I would never see her again. She died on April 24, 1988.

And if and when this ancient, very famous and historical landmark Sweet's should ever close, and (I hope not) become the end of an era, parting will be such great sorrow.

– *George Carloss, with Terry Walton,*
Seaport Magazine 1993, South Street Seaport Museum

John Noble's World ...
Down East Schooners Picking Up Coal

TODAY – John Noble's world (1972) is the heart of the Noble Maritime Collection in Staten Island.

To go to Staten Island, of course you board a ferry. Jim Kirk, Norma Stanford, and I did this one rainy September evening to visit John Noble aboard his barge in Port Johnston, across the Kill Van Kull from Staten Island. We had made the trip before when we used to walk the unexplored waterfront, thinking to find something like South Street Seaport in some corner.

Our journey started in the plastic and concrete surroundings of the Ferry Terminal (which someone someday should make a celebration rather than an apology for the City's relation to the harbor from which it was born); it ended in far more humane surroundings, near the sewage works and oil storage tanks of the foreshore of Bayonne. There, John A. Noble put the deckhouse of an old steam yacht aboard a barge and it served as his studio, where he recorded the processes of life and change in the world of schooners, tugs, barges, and old hulks retired from the high seas.

The hulks of three old five-masted barkentines guard this corner of Port Johnston. A collection of small summer cottages, walkways, and modest boats for weekend fishing has gathered here since World War II.

"At first," says Noble, "I was the only one living here, for about half a mile. Now we have people, and I've learned to live with them, you know. Or they with me."

He started his waterfront career in the mid-1920s. As son of the famous painter John Noble (1874-1934), he knew the artistic communities of Paris and Provincetown. But the latest cry in the battle of art for art's sake meant little to him. It was the life of the waterfront that drew him on as an artist, advocate, and interpreter of the life of the muddy foreshores, the men and the boats they work in. He takes pride in his craftsman's approach to this task. During the evening he picked up an adze to show Norma how you could make a shaving thin enough to see through with an easy stroke against an old hunk of weathered wood.

He talked of change in the harbor. When Noble came to it there were still big Down East schooners picking up coal from Port Johnston, and bringing in timber for pilings and other use. There were occasional deep-sea square-riggers still sailing. And there were many more craft of all descriptions than there are today; over 500 tugs, often sailed by individualist owners battling and bargaining for tows, not always gently; canal boats; and at least one Hudson River schooner, the *Isaac Sherwood*.

"It's changed so fast," he said, "there wasn't time to do more than begin to record it all. I could have spent a lifetime easily with those tugs – I used to go out in them, you know, the men were kind to a crazy fool. And I sailed a little in schooners where I could do a piece of work. I tried to catch the schooners as they passed."

– Peter Stanford, *South Street Reporter 1972,*
    South Street Seaport Museum

Art by John A. Noble (1913-1983) "Wreck, Studio, Artist and 2 Barrels or 3 Barrels and 2 Wrecks or 3 Wrecks and 2 Barrels," lithograph, edition 300, 1977 (courtesy Noble Maritime Collection).

★ *Changes with time – Only a few disintegrating timbers remain of the proud schooners and barkentines of John Noble's world a generation ago. But the ships are faithfully recorded in John's lithographs in the Noble Maritime Collection's Snug Harbor Center, Staten Island. Noble Maritime regularly takes young students out to draw their own impressions of harbor landmarks and other discoveries. Details, page 175 and www.noblemaritime.org.*

Frank Braynard –
A Tugman's Sketchbook Captures Our Harbor

Frank Braynard, the cheerful, irrepressible artist from Glen Cove, Long Island, was 90 years old not long ago and smiled broadly throughout his birthday celebration aboard South Street's square-rigger *Peking,* well-wished by a deckful of friends and family. His sketches have charmed many, his list of books is lengthy thanks to his love of liners and their welcome in our harbor, and he is known for great work years with Moran Towing, South Street Seaport Museum, and the Op Sail celebrations that he founded and caused to happen, gathering many to help him along the way. The Internet has 225, 000 listings for him thus far as artist, author, maritime historian.

Frank and Doris at his 90th birthday party aboard Peking . . .

I worked with Frank on many a project and remember with delight his constant response when asked how he was faring: "Never better!" And always said with a smile in his eyes. Frank Braynard, most recently Museum Curator of the U.S. Merchant Marine Academy of Kings Point, died in December 2007, beloved to a lifetime of maritime friends. Here are some Braynard words and some Braynard sketches – a mere sampling of this good man's lore in art and thought.

– *Terry Walton*

"New York Harbor is a dream setting for sketching . . ."

Ships are the largest moveable man-made objects. Their size, strength, unity and ability to withstand the elements, to shelter their crews, to serve – these attributes create for them almost human character. Ships live. ★ The excitement of watching a ship in motion, the high drama of the lives they live, the glamour of the seas and of their far-away destinations, these, and still other attractions impossible to define, all these make ships one of life's great objects to draw and paint. . . . New York harbor is a dream setting for sketching. The water itself in all its constantly changing surface patterns is a perpetually demanding and difficult subject. Every foot of the port's 600 miles of improved waterfront offers the sketcher a scene of new interest. Every boat, from water taxi to liner, is begging for the pen's attention. What better platform than the deck of a tug, which by its nature must go everywhere, serve all.

– *Frank Braynard, in* A Tugman's Sketchbook, Pen and Ink Impressions of New York Harbor *(John De Graff, Inc., 1965)*

Moran tug, ocean liner, and freighter from Tugman's Sketchbook.

Capt. Brian McAllister . . . Harbor Patriarch

The view from Brian McAllister's corner office on the twelfth floor of 17 Battery Place can take your breath away: You feel more immersed in New York harbor than looking out over it.

From the six windows of Brian's office, Governors Island dominates the foreground, while the Verrazano-Narrows Bridge and Staten Island mark the horizon. In the middle distance the Upper Harbor teems with ships, tugs, ferries, barges, yachts, and sailboats on a late weekday afternoon. To the left, lies the entrance to the East River; to the right, lies the Hudson River. Brian, the president of McAllister Towing and Transportation, oversees a fleet of 85 tugboats that operate from Maine to Puerto Rico, and runs the Bridgeport to Port Jefferson ferry as well. He is the fourth generation of McAllisters to run the company, starting with Irish immigrant James McAllister who moved his family into the Five Points slums and started out with a single sail lighter in 1864.

It's a long way from sail to 6,000 horsepower tugs that can turn on a dime and handle 150,000-gallon oil barges, and Brian has seen and done most of it. We were curious about how the world looked from his office windows.

Q How long have you had the view?
A Since 1984, but the McAllister company has been in this building since 1955.

Q Do you look out the windows to spot your boats?
A If I want to know where my boats are, there are better ways to find out. Something called "A.I.S.," for example, which shows where each boat is on a computer screen. But I do enjoy looking out at the various and sometimes new or strange vessels that go by.

Q Do you get distracted by the view?
A No – I know all the boats, and I'm used to it.

Q What's your earliest memory of the harbor?
A When I worked as a kid on our boats it was entirely different. The boats were steam pow-

ered, and there were finger piers on the Hudson and East River. As a tug captain I would spend all day digging barges out of the piers – lighterage barges that carried coffee, fruit, produce, pig iron, just about anything. The steam boats had a maximum of 600-900 horsepower. Compare that to today's boats with 6,000 horsepower and more, and that gives you some idea of the difference.

Tug Helen McAllister *(above) is now an historic exhibit at South Street Seaport Museum, where Brian serves as trustee.*

Q *Do you have a favorite time of the day for looking at the harbor?*
A No favorite time, but I'm always looking for interesting things. Like a new tugboat, or I see a very old boat go by. The tall ships are fabulous – but I usually see them from one of our tugs because we go out to see them. I live in Peter Cooper Village and my living room looks over the East River, so when I go home I can look at the water over there too.

Q *What's the most amazing thing you've ever seen in the harbor?*
A My father once drove me down the old West Side elevated highway and suddenly he stopped the car right on the highway. "Brian, look at that!" he said. It was the *Normandie*, rolled over onto her side and still smoking. It was the most beautiful, massive ship, the fastest liner afloat, being converted to a troop ship in the early 1940s when the fire broke out, and the fire department just poured water into her until she rolled over and sank. It's hard to forget that scene.

Q *What changes have you noticed over the years?*
A There's a lot less traffic, fewer ships going up to Albany or up the East River to New England ports. Short sea shipping has declined because it's a function of the high cost of stevedoring. On the other hand, shipping things like oil, scrap steel, coal, cement and sand and

gravel by barge is booming because there's no need for stevedores. Our fleet today works up and down the coast – eighty-five tugs and four barges, not counting the passenger-car ferries on the Bridgeport–Port Jefferson run in Long Island Sound.

Today, McAllister Towing operates an extensive fleet of tugs, barges, and ferries in the major ports on the U.S. East Coast and in Puerto Rico. In the Port of New York, the company handles a significant part of the sixteen million tons of cargo that move through the port each year. Capt. Brian A. McAllister is the president and a great-grandson of the founder, representing the fourth generation of McAllisters at the helm.

Four McAllisters of the fifth generation are also employed by the company. In recent times McAllister helped pioneer the development of the Kort Nozzle, Flanking Rudder tugs that dominated the 1960s and '70s. In the 1980s and '90s McAllister continued to modernize its fleet of tugs by building Z-drive tractor tugs with the latest firefighting equipment and capabilities. Today, the fleet includes twenty tractor tugs with four more being delivered this year. McAllister also owns and operates the Bridgeport & Port Jefferson Steamboat Company, which presently runs three large passenger-car ferries, each capable of carrying 1,000 passengers and 100 automobiles between Bridgeport, Connecticut, and Port Jefferson, New York.

– *Richard Stepler*

NOTE – Ship historian Norman Brouwer writes that the Helen McAllister *(see prior page) was launched on Staten Island in 1900, and christened* Admiral Dewey *for the hero of the moment. In less than six months she herself played a heroic role in the worst disaster in the harbor's history involving seagoing vessels. During a fire on the Hoboken waterfront that destroyed several piers and three German passenger liners, she succeeded in towing the largest German ship to safety, fought the fires, and rescued crew members trapped belowdecks on one vessel.*

The Hudson View
From Bill Baker's Office Window

At a meeting with Bill Baker of Channel Thirteen, I couldn't help commenting on the array of vessels passing by his window. His response was swift and telling. TW

Bill Baker and Walter Cronkite, old friends, at a Working Harbor Committee dinner.

Obviously I love my view. It's an inspiration and it's calming. And it gives me a sense of perspective, of history. I know some things about the history of this harbor, and I know that New York is what it is today because of its waterways. So that perspective is useful – that the crises of the moment are part of a continuum. I'm not at the beginning of the line, I'm not at the end. I'm part of something bigger.

My earliest acquaintance with New York harbor was when I was living in Cleveland, Ohio, near Lake Erie, and I saw the harbor in movies, and I fell in love with the water. So I began to study, romanticizing about rivers and oceans, and the obvious significance of the port of New York came up. It was years before I actually saw this harbor.

Two moments come to my mind, of my earliest New York harbor memories. One was in 1992, for the 500th anniversary of Columbus reaching our shores. I was then president of Westinghouse Television and somebody invited me out on a tug for this wingding event. I thought "That sounds like fun, there will be fireworks, it'll be a beautiful night." It was powerful beyond anything I could have foreseen. I was there with my wife, and I remember thinking, "this is a great moment in my life." It's engraved in my memory.

The other moment. . . . I was nearing my fortieth birthday. I knew how I wanted to celebrate it – somewhere on the harbor. So we chartered *Wavertree* down at the Seaport, invited fifty people including family, and had a catered event. Afterwards we went out sailing – was it on the schooner *Pioneer?* – a grand time. We never forgot that night, I know, because a number of employees brought their young children, today in their thirties, and they still refer to *Wavertree* as "Baker's boat."

The harbor vessels I think about the most? They are as follows – first, the most dramatic. Seeing this one was the most poignant, and later on in my years of ship-viewing: the U.S.S. *Comfort*, the navy hospital ship. I saw her coming upriver, near *Intrepid*, two days after the Towers fell on 9/11, having come up from Baltimore to help. She's all white, a thousand feet long with two big red crosses on her side. I was sitting at my desk with my binoculars – they're always right here, and *Jane's Fighting Ships* is programmed into my computer. I wanted to get aboard her and I did find a way. Aboard, I felt overwhelmed – at her size; to walk into this immense, seemingly thousand-bed hospital with eight operating rooms, as if you're walking into the biggest hospital in America. *Comfort* has a sister ship on the West Coast, another good name, the U.S.S. *Mercy*.

Other harbor vessels I care much about are the liners – particularly *Queen Elizabeth 2* and *Queen Mary 2*. Both of these ships, especially *QE2*, are ship-like, trim, nautical looking. They're beautiful. I fell in love with the *QE2* and later I was invited out on a cruise to Iceland and other points north. I lectured on that ship. To be in love with her and to be a lecturer on her maiden voyage, well, I sent ham radio QSL messages around the world. As for the *Queen Mary*, I was once invited, when she came in to New York, to go on a "Cruise to Nowhere." I wasn't about to miss that!

There are lots of other incredible harbor recollections. I don't know how to rate them – they're each so important to me and fit into different pieces of my life.

I remember when I first saw the tall ships. They inspired me, touched me, it was a bigger experience than I have words to explain. It was in the 1980s. I had arranged for Channel Thirteen to televise them, but we didn't have enough money to pay a host, so I volunteered to host the program. For five hours, I would be the main anchor at the booth at Governors Island. It came out fine and later I sold it, live, to be replayed on the Discovery Channel, but it's a funny story how it began.

How it began is, I had been all prepped, and there we were out on Governors Island, about to begin. And I said to myself, "Wait, am I out of my mind? I've never done anything like this!" I felt sick at the prospect. There was a huge fog, fairly rare but definitely there that day, and I thought, "Where are the ships? We can't even see them, and I'm going to talk for five hours about tall ships in the fog, and there are no ships?"

Well, one hour before our going on live, a crowd gathered, and someone waved. "Bill, do you need any help?" It was my friend Walter Cronkite. So I said, "Walter, would you mind just kind of hanging out with me?" He did, and this fear, this awful angst, just disappeared, the fog cleared, and the tall ships appeared. I simply forgot to be nervous with Walter there telling me sea stories. My daughter was there too, reading poetry about ships, and we were all loving it and having fun. What a day.

There are other harbor memories that are powerful for me. One of them is always Fleet Week. When I start seeing those big ships coming in, I check out the window with my binoculars to ID them. And other times, at night, it's spectacular – especially in early spring or late fall – when a cruise ship sails downriver with all her lights, heading out to sea.

I've had this office-window view of the Hudson – at the foot of 33rd Street – for about seven years. It was one of the reasons I was sympathetic to Channel Thirteen moving here, one of the things that drew me into making that happen. Next, I had to figure how I could get to be on the side that looks the right way, toward the river. And often, if I'm having a meeting and a cruise ship goes by, or a military ship, I just stop the meeting for a moment so we can all look out.

Today, right now, when I think of New York harbor I think first of the people I've met and learned to respect, people I love who care about the harbor too. There are lots of them.

– Office conversation with William F. Baker, Channel Thirteen/WNET, 2007

NOTE – Bill Baker oversaw a remarkable Channel Thirteen/WNET documentary called "Treasures in the Harbor – National Parks of New York City" – a pilot for a series celebrating the nation's 390 national parks, as the National Park Service approaches its 100th anniversary. Among NY harbor topics – Sandy Hook, Fort Wadsworth/Battery Weed, Governors Island, Castles Clinton and Williams, Liberty Island, and Liberty State Park. Details – Thirteen.org.

Tom Fox, Environmentalist & Water Taxi Man

Toss a pebble in the water and concentric rings appear and expand. That's how ideas seem to grow in Tom Fox's mind. Tom is president and CEO of New York Water Taxi – those sprightly taxi-yellow vessels that crisscross the harbor, connecting people and places. His ideas have changed our harbor for the good.

When Fox returned home to Brooklyn in the 1970s after Navy service in Vietnam, he explored his options and eventually took a trip back to New York that changed his life. He became a park ranger at our country's first urban national park, Brooklyn's Gateway National Recreation Area, teaching kids about the natural world. As Fox's interests and causes deepened, he was soon helping lead the Green Guerillas – environmental activists fighting for green space one small plot at a time. It wouldn't be long before he turned his attention to where land meets water – to the whole of New York harbor.

By way of background for all this, Tom's environmental education credentials are impressive: BS in biology from Brooklyn College, Loeb Fellow in Advanced Environmental Design from Harvard, and a list of related awards, board memberships, and published articles that runs off the page. By 1992, after varied environmental consultancies and directorships, Fox was heading the Hudson River Park Conservancy. His projects included plans and finances for the 4.5 miles of Hudson River Park, Chelsea Piers Sports Complex, the East River's Brooklyn Bridge Park, and more – each endeavor strengthening the city's public-access waterfront offerings today.

As the years passed, that initial idea of carving out recreational areas and gardens, like the pebble's rings, expanded. Says Fox, his mantra became "The working waterfront: you need a mix." True to his mantra, his headquarters are in Brooklyn's gritty Red Hook, at the Beard Street Warehouse, a still-functioning 19th century red-brick building that houses carpenters, parachute makers, and diverse other tradespeople. Gazing from his office window to an unobstructed view of the Statue of Liberty, Fox names Red Hook as one of his favorite harbor spots. "It's working. It's real. It's tangible. It smells and it moves."

Again, though, Fox soon went beyond his original visions. No longer content with bringing people *to* the water, he wanted them *on* it: "You know, it's great that you can walk along the edge, but you gotta get *in* it. You've got to feel it."

Fox started his intra-city water taxi service, New York Water Taxi, in 2002. A brief attempt with too little capital and "the wrong boats," he recalls, had failed five years before. But this time it worked. Today, his dream of connecting New York's previously disparate shoreline attractions such as the South Street Seaport Museum, Chelsea Piers, Governors Island, Water Taxi Beach at Long Island City, and Brooklyn's Fulton Ferry Landing is reality. His water taxis are the thread that links these jewels together.

Water taxi in familiar surroundings.

As the yellow boats with traditional black-and-white checks move forward, they honor the past. Fox names each vessel after his own unsung heroes of the harbor, from Brooklyn Cub Scout leader and environmental educator Michael Mann, to the tough-talking, chain-smoking environmentalist Mickey Murphy – who Fox says mentored him in the ways of fighting for park space.

Fox also credits the financial engine that keeps the water taxis afloat: support by real estate developer Douglas Durst. "Douglas is the reason all this is happening." Thanks to Durst's backing, New York Water Taxi has nine environmentally friendly boats in the fleet, with a tenth newly in service.

Today, for Fox, the rewards of running the water-borne cabs are both financial and emotional. "I'm still a missionary," he says with a grin, "and I'm trying to be a mercenary as well."

Reflecting on the missionary role, Fox recalls two boys and their fathers traveling from Brooklyn Heights to Rockefeller Park in downtown Manhattan. "I was on the boat when they went over to play, and I was on the boat when they came back. The kids are maybe four, five. They've got their little hands gripped onto the front rails. Their fathers are standing behind them holding their little sand pails. These kids are laughing and having a great time, their fathers relaxed behind them. And I thought, 'There we go. We got 'em. That's the next generation that's going to come back to the water.'"

The benefits of Tom's missionary-mercenary outlook are clear. Put a park on the water and the inboard real estate values rise, as evidenced by the gleaming new housing along Greenwich Village's westernmost edge. His viewpoint is, just as you need a mix of environments – working, recreational, and educational – you need a mix of people: the local community, government agencies, educational interests, and construction trades:

"I think that the way you get things done is to link together all the stakeholders. Everybody who's got a reason to be at the party should be at the party. And everybody should leave with a gift."

Fox cautions, though, that making change takes money, political will, and time. Botanist that he is – Fox's Brooklyn College degree is in field botany – he is patient to let his causes take root and grow. "You can't push an issue before its time. Give yourself twenty to twenty-five years if you want to make change." But now, Fox says, the harbor's moment has come. "It's time for the water. This harbor is magnificent. The city wouldn't exist if it weren't for the harbor." He stresses that using it makes logistical sense: "There's no traffic congestion on the river. No traffic lights. It is an assembled right-of-way we'll never see again."

What does the future hold? Tom Fox's vessels already do lots beyond ferrying (details www.nywatertaxi.com), and he does cooperative projects with the Working Harbor Committee, Metropolitan Waterfront Alliance, and other harbor organizations. But he plans to expand the water taxis' role still further by having convenient ferry service draw thousands of cars off New York City's streets. How? Use the nearly 40,000 underutilized parking spaces already in place at nine regional city, state, and federal parks, ferrying people from those locales right into the city.

He's also working on plans for a mixed-use maritime center with a commercial marina in Brooklyn's Atlantic Basin. Visitors could walk along the shore, have lunch or dinner, and feel the pulse of a waterfront operating on all cylinders. Maybe toss some pebbles of their own.

– *Hope Killcoyne*

Capt. Tim Ferrie,
Fourth Generation Sandy Hook Pilot

At 2 p.m. on a recent Monday morning, Capt. Timothy J. Ferrie boarded a 900-foot containership at Port Elizabeth, NJ, and piloted her safely out under the Bayonne Bridge, on past Staten Island to starboard, then under the Verrazano-Narrows Bridge and out to sea. He disembarked out at Ambrose Light. As a member of the United NJ Sandy Hook Pilots Association, it's his job to do exactly that: see ships in and out of New York harbor safely, night and day, in all weathers, all year round.

Tim Ferrie is a fully licensed "Full Branch State and Federal Pilot." Meaning, he has completed the requisite 7.5 years of apprenticeship, a written exam in which he must answer complex questions and draw the harbor from memory – and then serve as a deputy pilot for seven more years. It's serious business, this moving ships of all sizes and sorts in and around a harbor with infinite challenges of tide, traffic, and configuration.

Tim graduated from SUNY Maritime College at Fort Schuyler in 1978. He completed the requisite fourteen years of training, and is licensed for all waters of New York and New Jersey and tributaries. His merchant marine experience also includes two years as Third Mate on containerships to northern Europe and the Persian Gulf, and before that, service on a tanker to Antarctica. Impressive credentials, those.

In New York harbor today, to keep current, pilots must regularly check the Notices to Mariners and other up-to-the-minute sources, receive new harbor-change information from the association's director of training, and attend meetings about "harbor ops in the Port of NY-NJ." And for this ever-evolving harbor – shoaling here, dredging there, a navigation mark repositioned in last night's storm – the list of changes is long.

Highlights of Tim Ferrie's twenty-eight-year career are many. On the day he got his Full Branch License at long last, the pilot rotation had him up for the *Queen Elizabeth 2*. It was his first ship sailing out of the harbor with him in sole charge as a Full Branch Pilot – on a clear October day in 1992, early evening. Tim's voice still reveals his feelings of years ago: "Up on the bridge the *QE2's* Commodore Woodall asked me, 'Son, have you ever been here before?'

"I looked at him and said, 'No, Sir, Full Branch today.' That captain certainly understood the piloting system. He made a big fuss, gave me a beautiful autographed photograph of the ship, wished me a safe career."

Capt. Ferrie remembers piloting the 1,050-foot aircraft carrier *John F. Kennedy* on her last trip out of New York, two years ago, for Fleet Week in June. He was one of the pilots, boarding at the Hudson's Pier 88 passenger terminal: "You just walk up the gangway and go aboard, and are escorted to the officers' wardroom for a briefing with the navigator. There are hundreds of officers aboard a ship that size, and thousands of crew, so you're working with a team. And on a Navy ship, you oversee *them* doing the work; your job is to make sure that the orders they will execute will keep the ship safely in the channel. They go over the trip with you and take your advice seriously. There's little room to maneuver, and you both know it."

Ferrie doesn't work alone; no pilot does. His harbor interconnections are many and moment-to-moment: pilots association assignments, ship captains coming in and out of the harbor, tug captains meeting and maneuvering vessels of every conceivable sort. Then there's the Coast Guard and the Captain of the Port, all connected by VHF radio monitoring harbor traffic, the best anchorage considering time and tide, perhaps where a tanker will anchor to lighter off oil and lessen her draft so she can get to a dock to unload the rest of her precious cargo. The specifications for each job – vessel, draft, tide, destination, timing and traffic, weather, and lots else – keep varying.

Beyond these piloting tasks, Tim is active as president of the Marine Society of the City of New York. He presides at their meetings down at 17 Battery Place and responds, with other Society officers, to the needs of their many charitable and other maritime projects.

And well before the piloting tasks ever began, Tim states with unmistakable pride, "My dad was a pilot too, and his uncle and my grandfather before him, and on back. I'm the fourth generation in the business. My great grandfather was a partner in a pilot schooner, *NY Pilot Lobaut,* in 1882 – that's when he started his apprenticeship." Tim himself recalls that "from the time I was a kid, I always emulated my father. Growing up in Staten Island and summering at the Jersey shore, I learned from my dad how to row, how to fish and crab. Those were wonderful summers. I loved being around boats, that's all."

Tim likes to tell "one more little story" about the merchant marine's omnipresence in the harbor today. "Not long ago I was awakened as a pilot by an apprentice, a SUNY Maritime graduate. Then off I go to board the ship, a foreign ship we're bringing into port; the captain of the pilot boat is a SUNY Maritime graduate. And we meet up with the tugboat, whose docking pilot comes aboard to relieve me; he's one too. Likewise the stevedore who ties up the ship, and a maritime attorney who was there to see the captain. All six people involved when that vessel came into the port: all from SUNY Maritime at Fort Schuyler. It makes me proud."

In his twenty-one years as Sandy Hook pilot, Tim has not lost his awe at the responsibilities of his job: "It is fascinating. You climb up the side of a ship in a coat and tie, and that captain puts his trust in you to maneuver his ship. You are truly controlling the largest movable man-made object . . . and all on a handshake."

– *Terry Walton*

Capt. Thomas F. Fox –
Master Mariner & NY Harbor Man

Capt. Thomas F. Fox holds an Unlimited Ocean Master's License – meaning, he is qualified by the U.S. Coast Guard to command the largest commercial vessels anywhere in the world. Today, as a maritime arbitrator and consultant with years of open sea experience, he remains, at heart, a mariner.

Fox's years of maritime service have taken him well beyond New York's shores. "I'm proud of the skills I learned to enable me to navigate vessels," he states, recalling his merchant mariner training at SUNY Maritime College at Fort Schuyler, NY, and his later sea experience aboard American and foreign flag vessels. "We handled a variety of cargo – general cargo, steel,

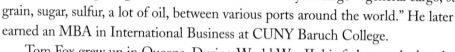

grain, sugar, sulfur, a lot of oil, between various ports around the world." He later earned an MBA in International Business at CUNY Baruch College.

Tom Fox grew up in Queens. During World War II, his father worked at the Bethlehem Steel Shipyard in Hoboken, converting cargo and passenger steamers into troop ships. The son knew well before high school age that he wanted to go to sea. He has since traveled afar both as seaman and as maritime businessman – including trips to Europe, South America, Africa, the Middle East, India, Pakistan, and the Far East. In the near-decade following 1967 he went to Vietnam (as a seaman) and Iraq (as a maritime businessman) six times each.

In the mid-'70s, while working ashore as Ship Operations Manager for a commodities trading firm, the company negotiated a three-year freight contract covering the movement of 500,000 tons of bagged sugar from Brazil to Basrah. About fifty ships were involved in the movements and he often flew to Baghdad and Basrah to sort out commercial problems and delays associated with discharging the vessels.

"My first commercial dealings with government officials and bureaucrats were in Iraq," he recalls. "Things were okay there then, but primitive technology-wise. You basically had to go to Kuwait to make an international phone call."

Fox is a recent past president of The Marine Society of the City of New York – a charitable and educational organization with a rich history. "The Marine Society is very old. It was chartered in 1770 when George III was King of England. One of the founding members was young Alexander Hamilton, who would become our first Secretary of the Treasury but was also a master mariner – a little-known fact. George Washington was an honorary member." When Washington made his farewell address to his troops at Manhattan's Fraunces Tavern, he was rowed across the harbor from New Jersey by a crew of Marine Society captains. Fox is rightfully proud of that, on behalf of the Society. In 1874, the Marine Society played a major role in the founding of the New York Nautical Schoolship, which subsequently became SUNY Maritime College.

As for his own New York harbor memories, Fox has a favorite one from his early days as a seaman. "Many years ago, 1960, when I was a cadet, I steered the Staten Island ferry one time from Staten Island to New York. I had just come back from my second sea cruise, and I went up on the bridge and introduced myself to the captain. And he said, 'Oh, yes. I graduated from SUNY Maritime too – well, in those days, in World War II, it was called Fort Schuyler.' So he let me stay up on the bridge. When we got safely away from the slip he took a few steps back and said, 'Here, you steer.' I'd already been to sea twice and knew full well how to do it, so I steered the ferry across the harbor. It was a thrill to do that – and remains so today."

Several years later, in 1965, he was Second Mate aboard a vessel that carried one of the last loads of grain from the Red Hook Elevator in Brooklyn. He also stood many watches as a port relief officer ("nightmate") aboard U.S.-flag general cargo vessels at various piers around New York harbor. As a Naval Reserve officer affiliated with the Military Sealift Command, he also attended training drills and stood relief duty watches at the Brooklyn Navy Yard, Brooklyn Army Terminal, Floyd Bennett Field and Military Ocean Terminal, Bayonne.

Capt. Thomas F. Fox has learned much about the world from his seafaring and maritime commercial experiences, and laments that Americans seem to become aware of other countries only when forced to don a uniform and do battle. "Experience tells me that American people don't understand geography." Once while visiting his daughter's school, he was disheartened to discover how little her schoolmates knew about it. His daughter's teacher invited him to give a lecture for those students and, taking the matter in hand, he requested some pull-down maps and a pointer, and went about giving a basic but thorough geography lesson. They had much to learn, and as a worldwide navigator and traveler Capt. Fox had much to tell them!

– *Hope Killcoyne*

Harbor Trips . . .
Living Aboard Solo,
Or Exploring Things With Family

Jerome Zukosky, Hudson-Harbor Dweller

Jerome Zukosky was born in Bayonne, worked locally for decades and lived elsewhere for a time, and newly returned, briefly, to New York and its ever-changing harbor. For this recent winter-to-spring visit he lives aboard his 42-foot cutter *Pilgrim* at Liberty Landing Marina, in New Jersey's Liberty State Park, just west of Ellis Island. For exercise he bike-rides in the park – "twelve hundred acres of mostly undeveloped land, not very crowded, a delight to be in" – or treks the two-mile walkway along the harbor, behind Ellis Island and the Statue of Liberty. The walkway surroundings differ every day and present his favorite harbor views.

In his earlier New York existence, Jerome lived in Manhattan, married and raised two children, and "made my living at the typewriter" as a reporter and feature writer for the *Herald Tribune* and the *Wall Street Journal*, retiring later from *Business Week* magazine. His transitory return to NYC brought the pleasures of both familiarity and things new. Among them – active out-on-the-water days with the Working Harbor Committee, helping with educational tours.

What's favorite about his Liberty Landing days: "I open the companionway doors each morning, and there are just four or five docks between me and the Hudson. Lots of masts, the whole cityscape of Lower Manhattan, it's fabulous – changes all the time depending on the light, and how the buildings reflect it. Sometimes I walk right down to the Hudson, and I see all the way up to the George Washington Bridge. And the skyline – you can see Manhattan's skyline all the way up to 72nd Street or so, west of Central Park." He likes author John Kouwenhoven's description of this "ragged and preposterously beautiful skyline." "I don't know if I'll ever get tired of the city's shores and harbor, with never-ending water traffic and the changes of weather and light and seasons. It's a magnificent affirmation of something profound, a testament to human drive."

Zukosky's favorite harbor-edge places? Years ago, the solace of South Street's Fulton Fish Market at four a.m. and eating at Sloppy Louie's nearby. And today, the ferry terminals and freight yards along the Hudson's New Jersey shore . . . and "that wonderfully restored Jersey Central Railroad terminal – whoever prodded the powers that be to restore it deserves a medal."

– Terry Walton

We'd Just Pick Up and Go . . .
A Mother & Sons Explore NY Harbor

Years ago when my children were little I heard someone liken living in an apartment to living in a box on a shelf. Not an image that readily evaporates, especially when you're raising two boys in a one-bedroom walk-up. So for us, the object of the game was to get outside. Just because I was a stay-at-home mom didn't mean we had to stay at home. After all, this is New York and there's so much to see.

Living as we do just south of Washington Square Park, the boys and I often wound up at nearby playgrounds, uptown museums, or friends' (larger) boxes on shelves. But we spent so much time along the spine of the island, my kids needed to experience the edges.

So we explored. Occasionally we went with others, but by and large we were a mobile threesome. I remember holding their little hands as we steadied ourselves on swaying piers. Or on the Staten Island Ferry, watching as they stared back at their skyline, mouths slightly open, hair whipped back ruler-straight in the snapping wind. Or standing comfortably close by on the deck of the *Intrepid* as a violently noisy Harrier plane hovered in place, frothing the water below.

But what do the kids, Jack now 11 and Lucas 15, remember of our many outings? What do they re-envision of countless trips to the grassy expanses of Hudson River Park, the long gray planks and tall ships of South Street Seaport, the Circle Line cruises, ferry trips, soccer games at Pier 40, and so much more?

Jack's first memory is what he *didn't* get to see. For starters, the *Intrepid's* pier-mate, the

U.S.S. *Growler*. "I wanted to go on the submarine, but I was five and you had to be six. I also remember a big red ship with fearsome teeth that I wanted to go on, but you and Lucas said, 'No, no, no.'" Luckily, the Water Taxi cruise around Manhattan was a hit. "There were a lot of thank you ma'ams coming back. And I remember going under this red bridge with lots of currents and some ship sank there with pots of gold. I remember passing lots of islands with cool houses."

And Lucas recalls excursions to the Hudson waterfront, a pedestrian haven that bloomed into vibrancy over the course of his childhood. On one trip to the Charles Street Pier, he remembers watching, heart in mouth, as his soccer ball *nearly* sailed over the fence and into the river close by.

Last year, the boys and I capped off years of trolling the edges of our island home with a flight above it all: a helicopter tour. I reckoned it would be like looking at a living map. Lucas, sitting up front, had doubts as we lifted off. "The pilot was in training, so at first I was really nervous. After a while I got used to it, but I realized it was actually more fun when I was scared." Jack: "It was a little scary because our pilot didn't seem like he had practiced landing a lot. But it was really cool seeing NY from above." All went well that day, thanks to both "pilot in training" and the pilot right beside him.

With assistance, the boys do remember some of our numberless other harbor explorations – a birthday party aboard the *Wavertree*, diligently filling out pretend passports at the South Street Seaport Museum, or how in 1996 an exhibit about the *Titanic* at the Seaman's Church Institute sparked curiosity, launching a year of study at nursery school. I wish they remembered more, but memory is like water, washing over itself and leaving new treasures on the shore.

– *Hope Killcoyne*

Vessels – Tugs, Tankers, Ferries, Containerships, & More

I am amazed by the vessels! Surely it has ever been thus, for harbor-gazers. My own ship investigations have been mostly by geographical happenstance: we lived for a time on the hills of Brooklyn, just south of the Brooklyn Bridge and above the Promenade, thus overlooking the tug-busy East River and Lower Manhattan, Governors Island, and the Statue of Liberty as well. From our Brooklyn window I saw Capt. Doheny's green-hulled tug *Brooklyn* at Pier 2 day after day. I watched the graceful grey-hulled *Newtown Creek* head upriver to her morning's work. And, freighters with exotic round-the-world names unload their cargoes with stevedores and shipboard cranes (these were pre-containership days). Further out I could see the yellow-hulled Staten Island ferry go back and forth in all weathers, and tugs churning their barges cross-harbor or upriver through Hell Gate to the Sound. South Street Seaport Museum, where I worked, was just across the river, with *Wavertree's* tall masts and *Ambrose* Lightship's red hull the anchors of my view. Well, as editor of South Street's *Seaport* magazine, why not write about all this? So I called various places – the EPA, the Coast Guard, the Port Authority, and the answer was always – thanks to the esteem in which the Seaport Museum is held – yes, come along. ★ More recently, of course, came Hidden Harbor Tours, The Great North River Tugboat Race & Competition, and an amazing tour of a Port Elizabeth containership terminal – all thanks to dedicated harbor souls on the Working Harbor Committee. *TW*

9 Notable Harbor Vessels – Each With Her Story to Tell

Steam Tug *Pegasus*

For ninety years, the handsome steel 1907 103-foot steam tug *Pegasus* worked actively in NY Harbor, first moving vessels and barges for her owners Standard Oil. Now she has a new job: educating the public about the unique environment of her harbor. *Pegasus* has undergone nearly five years of restoration work – with eighteen months in the shipyard for work funded by a matching grant from the NYS Office of Parks, Recreation and Historic Preservation. With the help of New York Landmarks Conservancy, New York Community Trust, and other corporate and foundation support we got through the shipyard experience. More about the shipyard work is on our website – www.tugpegasus.org. ★ We have worked with teenagers since 2002. The Maritime Adventure Program is one of many programs envisioned to bring people to the water and to their city's history. It's great to see people feel ownership of a waterfront that has been closed off for so long.

★ The tug *Pegasus* will be soon transformed into a living museum. With non-profit status, a listing on the National Register of Historic Places, and a

TUG PEGASUS

Pegasus students hard at their harbor tasks.

charter from the University of the State of New York issued eight years ago, the Tug Pegasus Preservation Project is close to realizing its mission of interpreting the tug's role in the city's maritime history, and of how tugs and the harbor are vital to our existence today. – *Capt. Pamela Hepburn, Tug* Pegasus

3-19-2007

JOHN J. HARVEY 75 ANNIVERSARY

Harvey *students . . . and harbor celebrations.*

Fireboat *John J. Harvey*

"Rarely is an historic landmark, honored for its past deeds, called upon to make an heroic contribution to the present. The 70-year-old fireboat John J. Harvey *and her crew did just that. . . . "*
– Sea History Gazette, September 2001

The work of the fireboat *John J. Harvey* on September 11 exemplifies the stories of all who helped – whether as on-land rescuers, as skippers and crew, or as brave and caring individuals. ★ The *Harvey* is as old as the Empire State Building and the George Washington Bridge. She retired in 1995 from active service as a NYC fireboat and remains the harbor's swiftest large fireboat and the oldest as well. On the morning of 9/11/01, her owners and crew met at her berth and headed south to the Towers to help. Joined by tugs, ferries, and other vessels the *Harvey* helped evacuate crowds stranded at the Battery sea wall to carry them north to Pier 40 and safety. She was soon asked instead to join other fireboats and pump seawater to the site; hydrants on shore were no longer working. ★ With other vessels, the *Harvey's* heroic role continued. Capt. Huntley Gill still tells the story – after days of pumping, her all-volunteer crew exhausted – help was still needed and the crew was polled by engineer Tim Ivory: "There's no other place we'd rather be than here." And so they stayed. Details on the *Harvey's* current harbor educational programs – www.fire-boat.org. – *HarborGuide, Working Harbor Committee*

★

Sludge Vessel *Newtown Creek*

The upper harbor looks calm now, as the sleek-hulled *Newtown Creek* leaves Manhattan in her wake at about twelve knots. In winter, however, her decks are often awash and her rails thick with ice from blown spray. . . . *Newtown Creek* – named after a once-clear stream in Queens – made her way down the East River past Governors Island and then out under the Verrazano-Narrows Bridge. It's a trip she takes about 300 times a year. From the bridge it's about twenty miles out to the sludge site marked on the chart. Nearing the site she slowed, as Environmental Protection Agency employee Richard Murphy lowered a probe to take samples at top, middle and bottom water levels.

Sleek-hulled Newtown Creek *heads to morning's work, nearly hidden against Manhattan shore.*

He repeated the procedure two more times, filling bottles, adding reagents, and calling out the results for recording. New York City has been testing its water for 40 years. . . . When dumping is prohibited, the sewage will be carried to treatment plants modified for the task. . . . *Newtown Creek* herself – with her graceful Philip Rhodes-designed hull, her oak, brass and mahogany trim, her specialized collection of valves, pipes and hoses – will carry sludge to the modified plants and will thus continue her life as a working harbor vessel, even as progress is made. – *Terry Walton, from Seaport Magazine 1987, South Street Seaport Museum*

★ *Changes with time – Ocean dumping moved to 106 miles offshore in 1987 and was banned in 1991. Sister vessels* Owls Head *and* North River *still do their harbor work, with* Newtown Creek, *carrying sludge to dewatering facilities for processing.*

★

Schooner *Athena* Opens the Museum

We were a strange crew, sailing in our old 43-foot schooner *Athena* toward a place where a vessel with fitted topmast hadn't been seen in half a century. Our destination was Pier 16, East River, next to the Fulton Fish Market on South Street, where draggers still came in. With my wife Norma and me were [square rigger sailors Archie Horka, merchant mariner and marine artist Os Brett, various city dignitaries], and my son Tom, who at age eight had become a great schooner aficionado and a good hand. . . . ★ It was a rawish Monday, 22 May 1967, and I remember things felt a little awkward aboard the schooner as she began to lean over sailing downriver close-hauled against the southeast breeze, with this mixed crowd aboard all dressed in city clothes. But her steady ways and easy motion in the roiled East River water soon made us all feel more at home, and with her divided rig with its multiplicity of lines to haul in or pay out, we made easy work of it. ★ The sail ended all too soon as we got the canvas off her, everyone hauling or slacking on different lines, and nosed into Fulton Slip to put our docking lines ashore. We straggled ashore to join a grand reception opening our new South Street Seaport Museum office at Fulton Street. . . . ★ Norma and I had to give up *Athena* a few years later, short of time and money to keep her going, but not before the Museum had acquired two great schooners, the *Lettie G. Howard*, a Gloucesterman of 1893, and the *Pioneer* of 1885. Both these vessels sail actively out of the Museum today, making the place a true home for schooners, as we had dreamed. – *Peter Stanford, Sea History Magazine, 1997*

★

"*Wavertree* sleeps though a winter morning . . ."

In this *Daily News* photograph, the 1885 square-rigger *Wavertree* sleeps through a winter morning in South Street, and an alert photographer takes her portrait, with the old ferry *Major General William H. Hart* and the rising buildings of the changing city just visible in the background. – *South Street Reporter 1972, South Street Seaport Museum*

★ *Changes with time – Today,* Wavertree *is the centerpiece of the South Street Seaport Museum fleet. She is newly celebrated in a booklet of paintings by the renowned maritime artist John Stobart, published by the National Maritime Historical Society, and has received a substantial grant from the city toward her vital next steps in restoration.*

★

Wavertree enters New York harbor in January 1895, as captured in John Stobart's painting, and in dusky early morning at South Street pier nearly four decades ago in 1972.

Schooner *Pioneer* – Beautiful Necessity of Life

In 1885, when *Pioneer* was built, she was plainly utilitarian. She was built as a sloop to haul sand from the lower Delaware Bay to an iron foundry in Chester, Pennsylvania. The grace of her iron hull could almost be called incidental – the gift of tradition. ★ Like a good coaster she lived a long, useful life, as freighter, harbor tanker, and, later, as a self-powered construction barge, hauling rock and piles for construction of breakwaters and bulkheads. And when she was old – when patches welded over patches no longer kept the sea out – she was run up on the beach, like many of her sisters before her, and left. ★ There Russ Grinnell found her and thought her too beautiful to die. He poured money and love into her restoration, the work being done well by Gladding-Hearn Shipbuilding Corp. of Somerset, Massachusetts. When she was launched in May 1968, *Pioneer* was new again – a traditional coaster with the modern benefits of hydraulic winches and Dacron. Russ set her to hauling piles and equipment in his waterfront construction work, and she served well in her new job until his tragic death in April 1970. In

August she came to South Street. ★ With the help of a grant from the Vincent Astor Foundation and gifts from individuals and business

firms, *Pioneer* began a new career in the spring of 1971: teaching New York City kids something of the responsibilities and rewards of the sea. It could well be the most useful work a coasting schooner has ever done. – *Richard L. Rath*, Pioneer Lives, *c 1972, South Street Seaport Museum*

★ *Changes with time – Today,* Pioneer *is still an active member of the Seaport Museum fleet; she takes members and friends out for educational and evening sails in the harbor. See details of her earlier work for the Museum, and of Dick Rath's vision for South Street, page 24.*

★

The Floating Pool Lady... Long Awaited, Welcomed in Summer '07

A colorful card in early '07 quietly announced her arrival: "She's here." In the card, the 280-foot *Floating Pool Lady* towed downriver under the elegant Brooklyn Bridge. (It was clearly a photo op, as *The Lady*, a former cargo barge, actually arrived from refitting/building in Morgan City, Louisiana, via the Narrows beneath the Verrazano Bridge). Feverish months of preparation at Pier 2 Brooklyn would permit her heralded opening on July 4, 2007, in Brooklyn Bridge Park. Cheery swimmers of many ages could hardly believe their good fortune, splashing in seven sparkling lanes near home with Lower Manhattan's skyline jutting up right across the river. By first season's end 50,000 swimmers from all five boroughs and across oceans had swum in her cooling waters. ★ For me, Ann Buttenweiser's dream – for she's the dreamer who made all this happen – began

in summer '07, she was nominated for the Cooper Hewitt 2007 People's Design Award (she came in a close second) and won a juried honor award from the Washington, DC, based Waterfront Center. Today, *The Floating Pool Lady* completed winter berthing in Bayonne, New Jersey, and the City Parks Department arranged for her reopening in spring '08 near Baretto Point Park in the South Bronx. Details, www.floating pool.org. – *Terry Walton*

★

years ago when I read her research on New York's floating baths: slat-bottomed wooden enclosures holding river water, a welcome resource in the hot 19th century city. Rather a different idea from today's pristine water in palest blue pool walls, but a dream-fruition nevertheless! Ann achieved her project with years of impassioned effort and the newly formed not-for-profit Neptune Foundation to fund it. As a former barge, *The Lady* retains her industrial heritage attractively and the city is the grander for it. ★ Within months of her opening

Tug *W. O. Decker*

New York harbor tugboats have been built in a variety of shapes and sizes to carry out specific tasks. The small wooden tug *W. O. Decker* of the South Street Seaport Museum was built in 1930 as the *Russell I* by Russell Brothers' Newtown Creek Towing Company to move barges in the narrow waterway separating Brooklyn and Queens. Later she was owned by the Decker family of Staten Island. ★ Mary Decker operated the company out of her family's modest home in a

WATERCOLOR AT SSSM, JACK PUTNAM

only fully intact steam vessel in the harbor. The Manhattan-based Lilac Preservation Project (details, www.tugpegasus.org) is working to return her to operation to restore an example of steam propulsion to the waters where it was first successfully introduced by Robert Fulton two centuries ago. – *Norman Brouwer*

★ ★ ★

tiny community on the shore of the Arthur Kill, using her kitchen table as an office. Her husband and son ran the boat. ★ *W. O. Decker's* present owners keep her operational, to move smaller vessels of their fleet and take people on tours of the harbor. – *Norman Brouwer*

★

Lighthouse Tender *Lilac*

Since 1939 the United States Coast Guard has operated tenders that maintain the buoys and other aids to navigation crucial to safe functioning of the harbor. The lighthouse tender *Lilac*, now berthed on the north side of Pier 40 on the Hudson River, was built in 1933 for the predecessor agency, the United States Lighthouse Service, and went on to serve the Coast Guard until her retirement in 1972. She is the last surviving steam powered lighthouse tender in the country, and the

Intrepid Refits
& Re-Opens by Year-End '08

Major among recent harbor events was the aircraft carrier *Intrepid* departing her Hudson River/46th Street/Pier 86 berth – after relentless dredging to break her free from keel-miring mud – and across the Upper Bay into dry dock for refitting in Bayonne, New Jersey.

The whole thing happened smoothly with the help of powerful tugs whose crews knew exactly what to do. "The renovation process is going smoothly and we are looking forward to a grand return," says the Museum's executive director Susan Marenoff. "She'll be back and her Museum up and running again by fall-winter 2008, it is expected." The yields? Vital ones, among them essential attention to aircraft, superstructure, flight deck, propellers, and ultrasound examination of her 917-foot steel hull that so bravely weathered hard service in World War II. Interior renovations will be completed locally in Staten Island. Details – Intrepid Sea*Air*Space Museum, www.intrepidmuseum.org. – *Terry Walton*

★ *Changes with time – Long associated with the aircraft carrier* Intrepid *in her Hudson River career, Fleet Week is a celebration of sea services hosted each May by the city since 1984. Every year, Fleet Week begins with what is for many buffs the weeklong event's highlight: a parade of military ships up the Hudson accompanied by a fly-over. The ships anchor at berths around the city, and the public is welcome to board. The sailors, marines, and cadets explain exhibits, offer musical performances, and even conduct rescue demonstrations. Details – www.fleetweek.mil.*

Aircraft carrier Intrepid *heads for dry dock and major over-haul in Bayonne, to be ready for reopening in year-end 2008.*

Heading home to Pier 4
Brooklyn *backs out into the*
harbor. She's 105 feet overall,
draws nearly 14 feet, and her
1,200 hp GM diesel engine
turns a mammoth 8-1/2 foot
diameter propeller. Jacobsen's
Shipyard, Oyster Bay, built
Brooklyn *in 1959. . . .*
Captain Doheny at the helm
of Brooklyn.

★

"Listening to Capt. Doheny talk, thinking of those
mind-boggling quantities of liquid sugar, noting the
expertly polished brass in the wheelhouse, I looked out at
the harbor. Tugs, dredges, scows, lighters, sludge boats.
Containerships, ferries, tankers, liners. All in the charge of
captains and crews. So many jobs in this working place.
So many men tough and wise in the harbor's ways."

★

A Day's Work
Aboard the Tug *Brooklyn*

TODAY – Capt. Doheny's molasses tug Brooklyn *(1974) is long retired, but look for modern tugs pushing barges, maneuvering ships . . .*

Her captain and our harbor have been friends for half a century. Look for her in the summer's harbor-watching!

"We're on today?"

"We're on."

"OK, see you at the dock!"

Out the door to a 9:30 a.m. foregathering aboard the harbor tug *Brooklyn*, already two hours into her day's work. Spring snow and engine repair had twice cancelled plans to board, but now we were set. Sunny April, clear skies, choppy harbor, winds 10-20 knots.

Brooklyn is a fairly new vessel – built in 1959 – and is very handsome with upright profile of deckhouse and stack, graceful sheer to hull (rigged typically with truck-tire fenders), green and black colors with bright yellow trim. She works eight or nine hours a day for her owners The New York Dock Railway Co. shuttling railroad car floats back and forth from Brooklyn to various docks in New Jersey. She is a vital rail link.

At night she berths at Brooklyn's East River Pier 4, just across and downriver from South Street Seaport Museum. And it was from both Brooklyn and the Museum that I had seen her, and with editorial boldness telephoned to ask if please could I come aboard to do a story for South Street.

"Sure! When?" was the response.

★

"The first cargo for us was a 13-car 300-foot float of liquid sugar from Erie Basin, which is just south of Red Hook and the Brooklyn Battery Tunnel. The sugar was destined for the Penn Central Railroad in Jersey City. Each car held 16,524 hot gallons!"

★

The first cargo for us was a thirteen-car 300-foot float of liquid sugar from Erie Basin, just south of Red Hook and the Brooklyn Battery Tunnel. The sugar was destined for the Penn Central Railroad in Jersey City. Each car held *16,524 hot gallons!* Erie Basin smelled of molasses as we left it. Sucrest makes the stuff there, explained New York Dock's Superintendent

■ 63 ■

of Transportation Walter DeSheers, for distribution across the country by rail or truck.

Heading out toward the harbor we passed Todd Shipyard and the sad grey hulk of *Sea Witch*, one of the two vessels that collided and burned near the Verrazano Bridge last year. A vast chunk of her bow was simply gone.

In the wheelhouse Capt. Doheny sounded *Brooklyn's* whistle to announce our stern-first emergence into harbor traffic; mate Tommy McGreel, well aft as lookout, conversed freely with him via hand signals. Tommy and one of the deckhands walked casually between tug and car float, which were made fast alongside each other with impressive hawsers but were still no walk I'd take.

Out in the harbor and heading west Capt. Doheny talked of his fifty years on these waters: born in Brooklyn, raised a "canaler" (his father operated and lived aboard a coal barge), twenty-three years as harbor pilot and New York Central tug captain, an interlude running molasses up the Hudson with a little 300 hp tug, and the last nine years as *Brooklyn's* captain.

His reminiscences were lively. ("Now you take Pier A there, at the Battery. Why I remember Mayor Walker's yacht *Macon* leaving there all the time to greet important people coming in the harbor. . . .") And reminiscences in turn were interrupted by irrepressible comment: "See that Coast Guard 40-footer? Racing along? Big waste of taxpayer's money." Or, speaking of the loss of special skills in the harbor today, "Pilots today? You blow a whistle at 'em and they just look at you. It's all telephone now."

On we went, sturdy *Brooklyn* with her railroad cars, casually following and disregarding channel markers as we headed toward New Jersey. In the wheelhouse the Chelsea ship's clock sounded mellifluously. I asked who polished it and the other bright brass: "Me and the crew," he smiled. Proud captain.

Nearing Jersey City's 13 Bridge Capt. Doheny excitedly pointed out a pile of sand. "See that sand? It's dredged from off Sandy Hook, dumped here for landfill, and two weeks ago there were ducks, black ones, brown ones, must have been ten thousand of them, all feeding on the shrimps in the shallows.

"And on those pilings – over there – " he continued, "Every one of them had a duck on it, with his neck stretched up. That's the males calling the females, when you see that."

Thirteen Bridge was ahead now and we gently unloosened sugar cars and went nearby for cars carrying hydrated lime from Oregon, our return cargo. The lime would go into cement for construction of schools and housing in the city.

Jersey City's rail bridges are nearly all out of service and literally falling down, and Capt. Doheny commented sadly on them, and on how the harbor used to be. Great storyteller, that man!

Now he and Walter DeSheers talked business for a while. I understood nothing beyond a few queries about cargo, but their friendship for each other was clear: the coat-and-tied young superintendent with tide clock, CG 369 harbor chart, and the Port District land transportation map in his office, and the wise and loquacious older captain. Deliberately leaving the channel for a shorter route Capt. Doheny said, "We should be kicking up mud now, Walter. Have a look?" Of course there was none.

Listening to Capt. Doheny talk, thinking of those mind-boggling quantities of liquid sugar, noting the expertly polished brass in the wheelhouse, I looked out at the harbor. Tugs, dredges, scows, lighters, sludge boats. Containerships, ferries, tankers, liners. All in the charge of captains and crews. So many jobs in this working place. So many men tough and wise in the harbor's ways.

Soon we were back at New York Dock Railway's Bush Terminal, the lime safely delivered and still another car float shuttled to still another dock. Capt. Doheny brought *Brooklyn* in skillfully, quietly, nudging the pilings precisely enough to put his boss and friend Walter off balance for a moment.

They exchanged grins, and we went ashore.

– *Terry Walton, South Street Reporter 1974, South Street Seaport Museum*

Oiler Ernie Romain moves brass-handled telegraph in response to captain's commands, shown by red arrow on telegraph's face, thus in turn slowing or stopping engine. Ferry crew includes 13 men beside Chief Engineer Hiller and his oiler and 1st assistant engineer: abovedecks – captain, assistant captain, mate, and five deck hands, and belowdecks – second oiler, water tender, and two stokers. . . . Yawl Petrel, *hazy Statue of Liberty, and gull-topped piles interest passengers as we depart Manhattan.*

Belowdecks on the
Staten Island Ferry *Verrazzano*

TODAY – The Staten Island ferry Verrazzano (1975) is retired from service, replaced by modern successors with traditional bright yellow hulls.

Seasoned chief engineer Carl Hiller takes us through the vessel's engine room, pilothouse, and tight passageways belowdecks, on a summer day's run.

Hot! And only with practice could I make my exclamation to that effect "heard." We were underway on the ferry *Verrazzano*, down in her throbbing engine-room. Communication was, I learned, better accomplished with hands and face-words than with sound.

It was well over 100 degrees down there. Lined up pounding deafeningly to my left was a steam engine with six of the largest cylinders I'd ever seen or imagined – five feet tall at least, and with pistons splashing oil against thick glass crank-case windows placed at eye-height for constant checking. Chief Engineer Carl Hiller mouthed the introductions: 1st Assistant Engineer Matt Kreshock and Oilers John Saward and Ernie Romain from the engine room; Spencer Smith and myself from South Street. The pistons made huge, rhythmic engine sounds and seemed joyous in their work. *Verrazzano* had just departed her Manhattan slip.

"It was well over 100 degrees down there. Lined up pounding deafeningly to my left was a steam engine with six of the largest cylinders I'd ever seen or imagined – five feet tall at least . . ."

Once unwound enough to look around I saw amber lights, red lights, green lights, dials and gauges for vacuum, steam pressure, and boiler pressures, and everywhere brass. Polished. The place was clearly a source of pride for its men.

Verrazzano's steel hull is 269 feet overall, we learned, has a sixty-nine-foot beam, and draws about thirteen feet. She has propellers at both ends, which should have been obvious to me but was not, and each is five-bladed and twelve feet in diameter.

Verrazzano is one of the three steam ferries on the city's Manhattan–Staten Island run. She has two sisters, *Pvt. Joseph E. Merrell* and *Cornelius Kolff*, named after World War II war hero and Staten Island real estate man and historian respectively. All were built twenty-four years ago in Mariner's Harbor, Staten Island, by Bethlehem Steel. On the run too are three diesel vessels built eight years ago in Texas: *American Legion*, *The Gov. Herbert H. Lehman*, and *John F. Kennedy*.

Chief Engineer Carl Hiller mentions details of Verrazzano's *4,600 hp six-cylinder Skinner Uniflow steam engine, her original, now 24 years old and in excellent health. . . . From high pilothouse of vessel* Verrazzano, *which like all ferries now is double-ended and short-bowed, captain can see well for docking and steering. Less serious matters, like how skillfully a passing skipper handles his yacht, or marine radio chatter about the five fish just caught near Buoy 4 – as well as the ferry's technicalities – are discussed here by captain and crew.*

Matt and John laughed and told stories and enjoyed our responses, but their eyes were always checking things. And soon, well before I expected, the captain's commands rang down from pilothouse to engine room telegraph: Slow at first. Then in a bit Dead Slow, then Stop and Full Astern. The commands came so fast I couldn't follow them, but John knew what was coming and stood with hand on telegraph ready to match command with action. Identical telegraphs are used by captain and engineer; there could be no mistake. Gradually, pistons slowed, throbbing lessened, bells sounded, we were there. Manhattan to Staten Island in an eighteen-minute run.

In the near-silence now, Carl Hiller talked. "The run's generally like this – five miles at about fifteen knots. But when there's fog it takes much longer. We slow to six or seven knots, wouldn't you say, Matt? Fog's plenty dangerous in this harbor."

"Have you had collisions?" this bold reporter asked.

"Well, there was one," he acknowledged. "It was this ferry, none of us were aboard, it was years ago." The matter was finished.

"What happened?" I prodded. He explained, unwilling to assign blame or even to tell awesome tales about his sort of job. ("Nothing much like that happens to you directly down here," he had told me. "Most that happens is you lose pressure or the vacuum, and that's not too dramatic." I began to admire this harbor man's quiet way about his work.)

What had happened, we learned in not too many words, was a night-time collision ten years ago between the *Verrazzano* and a coastwise tanker. The ferry carried eighty passengers, sustained a six-foot hole in her side, made it to her slip despite flooded engine room and boiler room, and sank to her main deck. And that type of accident was rare indeed. Radar and radio, dials and gauges, Jingle Bell, Cow Bell, and Gong commands set forth on a wall chart against the day the telegraph fails – everywhere around us were devices for safety.

Now the telegraph sounded again and we were underway for the return trip. An indicator's bright red arm now swung over to read: "To Manhattan." Men down in the engine room for eight-hour shifts need to know unequivocally the ferry's direction; imagine the chaos otherwise.

Out on deck Carl Hiller spoke affectionately of still another vessel – the *Mary Murray*. She's nearly forty years old now and her future is uncertain. Her loss from the run last year seemed to stand for the loss of other things too, harbor things that even now the younger ferry men don't know. Carl drew pieces of knowledge and memory out of his sea life – from time as machinist's mate on the Navy tanker *U.S.S. Trinity A.L. 13* in 1940-44, with the Asiatic fleet, to construction man on Ellis Island, to rigger of tankers and tugs in Mariner's Harbor shipyards. His grandfather was a canaler with steady Hudson River runs down from Buffalo, his father a Navy man with long shipyard years. Carl himself recalls grand swims off of Shooter's Island docks in the 1930s. His Department of Marine and Aviation work began as a stoker twenty-two years ago. He's been a chief engineer for the last thirteen.

Belowdecks next in boiler room and engine room again the chief engineer showed his visitors patiently – and bemusedly it seemed – Davis Condensate Filter, 375-lb pressure boiler feed pump, 300 kw electric generator, fuel-oil tanks, and fire pump, rows of boiler gauges, and high- and low-suction cooling-water-system valves. The cooling-water strainer needs periodic cleaning to rid it of debris and surprising harbor-water intruders like shrimp, killi, and crabs!

Interspersed with the technical things were some more stories, most of which were comprehensible despite the engine sounds' competition. But one story dealt, as it happened – and apocryphally – with the old days when men judged the ferry's direction by which way the horses loaded on the main deck were facing. ("Horses?" I wondered. "How do they figure here?") There I was idiotically nodding and nodding, straining to hear over the engine's enveloping throbs, hoping to understand this serious tale pretty soon, and asking knowledge-

---
★

"Now the telegraph sounded again and we were underway for the return trip. An indicator's bright red arm now swung over to read: 'To Manhattan.' Men down in the engine room for eight-hour shifts need to know unequivocally the ferry's direction; imagine the chaos otherwise."

★

Bells, lights, and gauges in Verrazzano's *engine room.*

able questions. But when the shaggy story was over, all that happened was that Carl Hiller smiled a pleased smile at having led his earnest listener down the engine-room path.

We completed what must have been six runs that day, and soon Chief Engineer Hiller needed to attend to other work. So up to the pilothouse we went for the final docking at the Battery. Out in the harbor we had sounded the steam whistle three times in salute to the new African cargo ship *Lumumba*. It was a glorious sound. And she was surrounded by high-spraying fireboats and all sorts of escort. Nearing the slip I watched Captain Donaldson and Carl Hiller talk easily of both technical things and family things. I listened raptly to Deckhand Jimmy Schneider's tales of rescuing a passenger from a fall overboard several years ago. I watched Captain Donaldson's second-natured handling of *Verrazzano's* fine mahogany wheel and felt the vessel nudge the slip's hard greenheart piles firmly, perfectly.

Passengers queued behind gates on the deck below to go ashore. Passengers from ashore surged aboard. And of course now it was time to get ashore ourselves lest we depart again. . . .

Days later, watching the yellow ferries in their back-and-forth runs, I saw a summer squall build up behind Manhattan. Black sky overtook blue. Harbor water lost its sparkle and turned white-whipped grey, as wind came and brought with it walls of rain. Warning signals and lights went on at the Battery. Tugs and a small brave sloop nearby turned on masthead lights, and the ferries turned on their lights too. Back and forth they went, through gale and torrent and no visibility at all. And when it was over back and forth they still went. I wondered if Carl Hiller was on the run that day.

– *Terry Walton, South Street Reporter 1975, South Street Seaport Museum*

NOTE – *The Bridge (Verrazano-Narrows) and ferry (Verrazzano) differ in their spellings. See the ferry's nameboard, page 68.*

"We were very tired, We were very merry . . ."

We were very tired, we were very merry –
We had gone back and forth all night on the ferry.
It was bare and bright, and smelled like a stable –
But we looked into a fire, we leaned across a table,
We lay on a hill-top underneath the moon;
And the whistles kept blowing, and the dawn came soon.

We were very tired, and we were very merry –
We had gone back and forth all night on the ferry;
And you ate an apple, and I ate a pear,
From a dozen of each we had bought somewhere;
And the sky went wan, and the wind came cold,
And the sun rose dripping, a bucketful of gold.

We were very tired, we were very merry,
We had gone back and forth all night on the ferry.
We hailed, "Good morrow, mother!" to a shawl-covered head,
And bought a morning paper, which neither of us read;
And she wept, "God bless you!" for the apples and pears,
And we gave her all our money but our subway fares.

– "Recuerdo," by Edna St. Vincent Millay

★ *Changes with time – On a recent July morning, there were no free seats at all in the new Staten Island Ferry terminal, Manhattan side. Crowds surged in from the subway adjacent. Young boys in red team shirts walked in line to board, watched over by their camp counselors. Bicyclists gathered in their designated pre-boarding space. Other passengers-to-be strolled, strode, skated to board too. Babies, new parents, grandmothers, businesspersons, everyone was there, soon to board the* John F. Kennedy *or the* Samuel I. Newhouse, *whose flags were snapping in the wind. On the return trip, a digital readout said "Welcome to Whitehall Ferry Terminal." And up on the wall over it all, in largest imaginable letters, were the words of "Recuerdo": "We were very tired, we were very merry . . ."*

"Lashed alongside to starboard is the Gelberman's *collection device — a floating V-mouthed contraption with a net strung underneath it. By mid-morning, it is already half full of crates, planks, tires, and other gifts from pier and shore."*

Crewmen maneuver an unwieldy waterlogged plank in the hydraulic claw's grip. The plank will lie across the stern until transfer to a barge, for burning, later that day.

TODAY – Gelberman (1981) is still in active service, with modifications to meet an expanded environmental mission. See Changes with time, below.

Drift Collector *Gelberman*
She's Brand New. What Exactly Does She Do For a Living?

The Drift Collection Vessel *Gelberman* is small as working harbor vessels go (85 feet – her fleet sister *Hayward* is 120 feet), but she is mighty. She looks like a tug and is even classified as one, but she is not a tug at all. She has a look of strength and no-nonsense assignment about her, but the nature of this work is not so apparent at first. Simply, the *Gelberman* spends every day of the year collecting our harbor's flotsam and jetsam. She's the newest in the U.S. Army Corps of Engineers eight-member fleet of drift collectors, survey boats, and patrol boats that keep New York's navigable waterways navigable.

On a routine day during this her first summer the *Gelberman* leaves her Caven Point (New Jersey) berth at 7:45 and heads south toward her morning's work. Well off to starboard bright blue Hudson River trap rock tugs are bringing their barges eastward around the Battery, perhaps headed for East River or Long Island Sound construction sites. The Coast Guard's graceful cutter *Gallatin* lies at her Governors Island dock in Buttermilk Channel.

On board the *Gelberman*, a thriving potted plant of unknown name takes sun on the after-deck. "I put it out to get some fresh air," Capt. Richard Gaudreau explains to a visitor on board. "It was locked up so its only sunlight was through a porthole. It's our mascot."

Lashed alongside to starboard is the *Gelberman's* collection device – a floating V-mouthed contraption with a net strung underneath it. By mid-morning, it is already half full of crates, planks, tires, and other gifts from pier and shore.

The day's routine tasks are determined each morning by wind and tide, Capt. Gaudreau notes. He is a soft-spoken man whose explanations are patient, in a manner acquired in eleven years of Coast Guard and Corps of Engineers service. Debris tends to gather in "streaks" – the lines formed by tidal rip edges and clearly marked by white frothy strips in the water. From tide and current charts and from the way the wind heads the flag at Caven Point, Capt. Gaudreau knows where streaks will be, so he now heads directly for the next one. Mate Brian Aballo – at age twenty-four the youngest member of the crew – runs the *Gelberman* right along the streak. He makes only slight maneuverings to position the collector's mouth

The Gelberman *has an icebreaker bow – raised and strengthened – for year-round harbor work. Her starboard side is reinforced with steel plates to withstand the working of the 25-foot collection platform lashed alongside.*

properly. Out on the walkways of this odd appendage, two deckhands use pikes to guide an errant forklift pallet into the net. The pikes resemble boathooks, but each has a lethal threaded point that screws into the quarry and must be deftly turned before it'll come out. Ancient weapon with a modern use, a crewmember observes.

The *Gelberman's* crew is a mixed, comfortable team – six men age 24 to 55 or so, one with a nine-week-old son named after his grandfather, one with grown children soon to leave home. They've all got Corps of Engineers or other sea experience, and all find this New York harbor work worth doing. Only when asked by a visitor does one of them speak of the hardship of winter work, the dreariness of rainy days, the shock (which does not leave) of finding awful things like the bodies of people and dogs. Although the crew are new together – the *Gelberman* was christened in May at South Street's Pier 16 – they are well attuned to each other. Jokes are told. Family stories are exchanged.

Interrupting one story now comes a radio message from the *Haendel*, a Corps of Engineers patrol boat that investigates calls from ships regarding special debris sightings, and that makes her own searches as well. This time, the *Haendel* has found a submerged boat, kept from the bottom only by the foam flotation under its seats. She's towing it in and meets the *Gelberman* beneath the Verrazano Bridge. Alongside, chains are lowered from the *Gelberman's* stern crane. Its fierce-looking claw closes and lifts the boat by its chains, up and onto the afterdeck. The boat is small enough – about a sixteen-footer – that resting athwartships it leaves the deck free for other work, and does not project out over the gunwales. (A gasoline-powered Homelite saw on board would remedy that otherwise.) The boat has been stripped and holed, perhaps because the prospect of storage costs in the fall was too much for its owner. For a boat without that abandoned appearance, Capt. Gaudreau will also ask the Corps of Engineers Harbor Supervisor to track down its owner, and assess him for its removal.

After a run down one or two more tidal streaks the collector is nearly full: newly added are chunks of piers, more tires, plastic bags, beer cans, a tennis ball, a bright orange feather that must have a story of its own to tell, and a hefty tree branch. "After storms and full moons we get drift like crazy," Chief Engineer Tony Hans says, alluding to floating trees and branches, and with a grin at the lunar irony of his words. There was even a dead whale in the Kills off Staten Island last year, he recalls. *Hayward* found it beneath the Goethals Bridge, and towed it to Caven Point to await examination by Yale University scientists.

Above and inset: Deckhands John Tierney and Georg Lazides guide debris into the collector's jaws and barely submerged net, each using a boathook-like piece of equipment called a pike.

Soon the *Gelberman* will head in to discharge her motley cargo onto a barge and head back out for the afternoon. That night her crew will go their separate ways ashore and be aboard for the next day's harbor work. And that will be, as they take some pride in saying, unpredictable every time.

– Terry Walton, Seaport Magazine 1981, South Street Seaport Museum
Photographs by John Senzer

★ *Changes with time – Nearly two decades later, the* Gelberman *is still clearing debris from the harbor. Modifications to her crane allow more versatility in grabbing garbage, and an expansion of the vessel's mission now includes "floatables" – smaller pieces of garbage (such as medical debris) that are environmental hazards but not necessarily threats to navigation. A recycler sorts through the debris, reclaiming mostly wood, and the rest is sent to landfill. Sister vessel* Driftmaster *participated in the Working Harbor Committee's early Working Harbor Days, for inspection by the public.*

COURTESY U.S. COAST GUARD

Ambrose Light Tower, seven miles out to sea in approach to NY harbor . . . Tower crewmembers in the 1970s . . . Helicopter transport lands atop the Tower . . . Ambrose lightship circles her successor on retirement day, 1967, signal flags saying "I am not in my correct position."

Ambrose Tower –
Keeping the Light to New York Harbor

TODAY – Ambrose Tower (1993) is no longer manned and is being dismantled after being rammed by a tanker. See Changes with time, below.

Six men live seven miles out to sea on Ambrose Light Tower, off Long Island and Sandy Hook, manning the light that guides ships into New York. What's life like way out there?

Ambrose Light Tower is one of New York's near-secret forces, for it affects all city dwellers' lives but nobody much knows about it. It is a Texas-tower sort of structure that marks the harbor's treacherous southeastern entrance, up Ambrose Channel, guiding laden ships into our piers from all over the world. Every imaginable kind of goods comes by its station in ships, as it has for a hundred years and more, for use by people in city and suburb.

The Tower stands ten miles east of Sandy Hook Lighthouse, in New Jersey, and seven miles south of Long Island's south shore. It is often visible from these beaches, looking rather like a long-legged chair. Six Coast Guardsmen man the Tower in two-week-on, one-week-off shifts. In their work these men maintain a harbor navigation tradition begun in 1823 by *Sandy Hook*, the first ship to keep the light outside New York harbor. More than forty other lightships have been stationed on both U.S. coasts since then, but only one – *Nantucket* Lightship – still survives the efficiency of the modern light tower today.

Red-hulled *Ambrose* Lightship – one of the Tower's several predecessor vessels on the station – was the first member of South Street Seaport Museum's fleet of historic ships. It seemed thus an almost proprietary request when historian Norman Brouwer and I asked Coast Guard officials on Governors Island if we could take the trip out to the Tower. "Be at Brooklyn Air Station at 8:30 Thursday morning 18 September," was the instruction. "It's a regular run."

At the Air Station at what to some is an ungodly hour we found helicopters at the ready, flags up and waving, and work well underway in hangar and office. En route we had passed "Independence Avenue," "Enterprise Lab," "Forrestal Road" – all resoundingly military, for the Coast Guard once shared Floyd Bennett Field with the Navy. We had also seen ducks and pheasant and lush dune grasses, attesting to the field's situation at the very edge of Jamaica Bay.

Inside the Coast Guard hangar, men on yellow mobile scaffoldings were examining helicopters. At the water's edge, gulls and little sandpiper-like birds searched for creatures left by

the tide. Other non-military sights were nearby – a red sloop lying waiting at a dock, inquisitive dogs, a jogger. All around was efficient early morning quiet.

Aloft at last and headed south out to the Tower we surely must have amused the pilot and crew with our excitement. Earphones and Mae Wests were apportioned. Sea rescue gear for the copter's other work – dye marker, cable splicer, space blanket, shroud cutter, knife – was all in place and labeled. In the distance offshore we soon saw the Tower – so tiny!

B anking into the wind we came closer, closer, and settled perfectly on the marks, black lines on a ninety-foot platform often out of sight of shore, well out on the Continental Shelf. As we disembarked I was struck with the isolation of the men who live here.

"Lie down or go inside," motioned the first Tower man we met. "Safety during the take off." The helicopter left quickly, we stood up in the new silence, and the Tower man introduced himself as MK1 Ted Hedrick, acting officer-in-charge of the Tower, who is forty-five and lives, we learned later, in Athens, Pennsylvania.

Games, television, and reading lend routine to off-watch hours. For exercise, the crew use barbells and other gear in the exercise room, or jump rope out on the helicopter pad. . . . the officer in charge gives a stir to lunch – the one meal a day when the crew are all awake at the same time.

Hedrick took us below – or downstairs as you say on this maritime but stationary structure. MK3 Paul Chiarky of Hopewell, Virginia, age nineteen, and PNMK Paul Johnston of Millville, New Jersey, age twenty, had finished cleaning up after breakfast. The three others of the Tower's crew were gone, on compensatory leave or ashore buying the week's supplies. Chiarky was about to make his rounds of radio beacon room, office, engine room, and light – part of his watch routine of eight hours on and sixteen off. There is a man on watch at all times, lest the vital light fail to send its six-million-candlepower beacon from dusk to dawn.

We all spoke awhile in the crew's lounge. On its walls hang oil paintings of New Jersey's Navesink and Sandy Hook lighthouses and of *Ambrose* Lightship herself, done thirteen years ago – in the Tower's first year – by a Coast Guard man with a pleasing talent.

Chiarky and Johnson showed us the billiard and pinball games that the Tower men pass the time with. ("When you're off watch and awake, you sure need something to do!") In each eight-hour watch the men make rounds every hour, and on weekdays do regular maintenance and housekeeping work during an additional four hours. But there are still plenty of hours left when other men would be home with family or friends. The games and television, books and magazines, and binoculars for ship- and people-watching play a part in every day's routine.

Hedrick listened while we spoke of our own *Ambrose* Lightship, and of our interest in examining the light that replaced the ones on our lightship's masts. The Tower sends a three-quick-flash-white five-second-silent light, we learned. It is so powerful that ships can see its flash when they are well beyond the horizon. And any human contact with its mechanism means a rather hasty, thorough electrocution. As we climbed toward the light, Hedrick pulled a switch that unequivocally cuts off its power. Next came a ladder-top hatch in the floor that, when open, creates a second complete cut-off.

The light is compact and awesome – three banks of upper and lower xenon flash tubes each backed by a vast aluminum reflector. These must all have just received their weekly polishing.

---- ★ ----

" 'What if it fails?' we asked. If ships rely so heavily on this light to find the channel they'd surely be in danger without it."

---- ★ ----

"What if it fails?" we asked. If ships rely so heavily on this light to find the channel they'd surely be in danger without it. There's standby power and a standby light, Hedrick explained. And auxiliary systems for the fog horn and fire equipment as well. If trouble comes, any other help is far away.

Chiarky was making his rounds now, and we went along. The layout of the Tower began to come clear, an oddly difficult achievement with the same ocean scene outside every window. The Tower has in effect five levels – the light tower, the helicopter pad, just beneath it the equipment room and the living and office accommodations, and below that the oil-rig-like understructure with its two levels of walkways connected by a spiral staircase. The staircase is, of course, primarily functional; it winds its way down around a Tower leg and offers secure footing to anyone going down to water level. But it is also an incongruously beautiful aspect to this otherwise stark structure.

The Tower itself was built in Norfolk, Virginia, and towed to New York on barges in the summer of 1967. Its legs stand in sixty-five feet of water and have been driven a further one hun-

Anemometer and vane yield wind speed and direction . . . as monitored at console. . . . Fishing yields blues in season. . . . "Mickey Mouse ears" stand ready for fog days, to protect crew from Tower's two-second blast every fif- teen seconds, heard three-to five miles away. . . . Oak chair on Tower's understructure is a fine place for ship watching, record-taking, and anticipation of life ashore. . . . In rounds, watchman lowers temperature gauge ten feet beneath the surface, and reports findings to National Weather Service.

dred seventy feet down into the sea bottom. It is built to be safe in one-hundred-twelve-knot winds and sixty-two-foot seas, which is of course a discomfiting specification to think much about. Up on the accommodation floor Chiarky signed a log in the office, where radio messages are sent and received, and where the officer-in-charge does his desk work. Next came the radio beacon room, where he signed again to confirm that the Tower's RDF transmitters and other equipment were functioning well. In the engine room Chiarky checked the three one-hundred-ninety-five horsepower G.M. diesels that power the light at sundown. And in an adjacent room, rows of giant batteries stood ready to provide its power should the diesels fail. Nearby, ranks of CO_2 cylinders awaited a danger that they all hope will never come: fire.

--- ★ ---

" 'The helicopters are grounded. We'll be sending a boat by 1400 hours' . . ."

--- ★ ---

Out on the understructure walkway now Chiarky checked a tide gauge and lowered a thermometer to check water temperature; he'll check anemometer and vane shortly and every three hours relay what he finds to the National Weather Service.

Watch chores complete, lunchtime at hand, we headed back to the lounge. On the way a glimpse at the Tower's bedrooms showed them to be paneled, comfortably furnished, and more dormitory-like than "maritime," whatever that term may mean when applied to what is, in effect, a very complex lighthouse on stilts.

In fact, the Tower simply isn't like any other structure except another tower. Men stand watches and the Tower is at sea, but it is not a ship. Men live on it in a kind of family orderliness, but their real families are somewhere else. The Coast Guard's compensatory leave schedule is liberal, Hedrick pointed out, because most men need that balance to this kind of life.

"The helicopters are grounded. We'll be sending a boat by 1400 hours," came the radio message regarding our return to shore later that day. Why grounded? Not the weather; the day's fifteen knots of wind were comfortable, the pilot had told us, and anything up to twenty-five knots of wind is even easier, because it tends to be stable to fly against. The trouble was some structural damage on one helicopter that was being checked on the others as well. So, awaiting the boat, we settled into backgammon and talk in the crew's lounge.

"When it's blowing out there, the Tower moves and the billiard balls roll," Chiarky announced with a grin. "And once when the heat went off in winter it got down to forty

Spiral staircase connects upper and lower under-structure levels, and is tough going in winter. . . . Slung from the Tower's cargo hoist, a hefty canvas bag takes up the last of the week's supplies brought out by a returning Tower man.

degrees in here," he added. "Try that sometime! And, when the fog's in and that horn goes for days you think you'll go crazy."

Chiarky is married and has a child and has been on the Tower for fifteen months, with three more to go in his tour. He concentrated on his backgammon game – and won it – but kept an ear cocked to the walkie-talkie that served as an intercom to the office radio. He was still on watch.

All three men knew something of the Tower's history, and that the first *Ambrose* Lightship was at our Museum. We exchanged our facts about both – that *Ambrose* had raised 2.5-million-candlepower lights sixty-five feet high on her masts and had a crew of sixteen, that the Tower sends a six-million-candlepower light from one hundred fifty feet up that can be seen for twenty-two miles – from beyond the horizon – and has seven fewer crewmen than the lightship did. And that when tower replaced ship in the summer of 1967, the final *Ambrose* (the fourth on the station, a successor to our own) hauled up her anchor and circled the Tower three times, her international code flags "P" and "C" – "Papa" and "Charlie" – saying "I am not in my correct position."

The boat was on its way for us. Hedrick came back from after-lunch solitaire and television news in his room, and we walked outside to wait. We watched one of the pilot boats standing off two miles or so, waiting for a ship that one of her pilots will take into New York. If a certain buoy five miles off from the Tower is not visible during the day in fog or poor weather, Hedrick explained, then the watch man turns on the fog horn and the light and hoists the storm-warning flags. Otherwise he just turns on the light an hour before sunset and turns if off an hour after sunrise.

Weather – of many sorts, Hedrick noted – can turn their otherwise uneventful days into something quite different. In dense fog the Tower cannot be seen and cannot, of course, move out of the path of ships, six hundred of which pass by every month. Lightships have often been rammed, and one was knifed amidships and sunk near this station in 1966. In storms neither helicopter nor boat can reach the Tower, so men scheduled for leave must forego it for a while. And if the weather calms by night the helicopter still cannot come, because it couldn't land out there near the blinding light.

The one time a helicopter did come at night, Hedrick recalled, was when a boat passenger sought the Tower's help for a serious cut in her neck, and Hedrick judged her life to be in danger. That night the main lights were replaced by the less powerful standby and flight-deck lights during the moments of landing and take-off.

Hedrick was speaking of the other Tower men now, in family terms. "The kids like to watch television things like Love Boat, but I like to see the news. Keeps me in touch." He likes Tower life, and had served an earlier tour and requested this second one. He had also served on an eighty-two-foot patrol boat in Vietnam, and knows what life on *Ambrose* Lightship was like because of still other service in *Umatilla* Lightship, out on the West Coast off Washington, in 1969. After retirement in a few years he'll build a place in Pennsylvania, so spends some Tower time reading all he can about solar heating.

The wind had built up swells below, we saw. The Coast Guard boat was visible in the distance now, racing toward the Tower. Nearing, the forty-one footer came stern-to at first and sent up supplies by canvas bag on a hook lowered from the Tower. Three batches and it was done.

People were more difficult cargo. The boat couldn't come alongside because of the swells and the height of the tide. Bow-in she came, then surged back, while two returning crewmembers jumped neatly up onto the Tower walkway.

– *Terry Walton, Seaport Magazine 1981, South Street Seaport Museum*
Photography by Alan Orling

★ *Changes with time – Ambrose Tower, rebuilt after being hit in 1999, was rammed by a tanker in November 2007 and sustained substantial damage to legs and stanchion. The Tower is being dismantled in 2008, replaced by a nine-foot-tall buoy with a powerful LED light. The buoy and other markers will be moved farther offshore, because the channel is being lengthened as well as deepened. The original Ambrose Lightship of 1907 remains an honored member of the South Street Seaport Museum fleet.*

A Guide to NY Harbor Vessels Today

East River, Hudson River, Newtown Creek, Brooklyn Navy Yard, Erie Basin, Atlantic Basin, Arthur Kill, the Upper and Lower Harbors with multitudinous basins and bays and bridges – New York harbor is a complex of interconnecting waterways, a highway system for working ships and boats that serve the surrounding New York–New Jersey cities. Here are some highway vessels you're likely to see as you explore the harbor, with a note about their jobs in our harbor and beyond. ★ With some representatives shown here and some not, I respectfully acknowledge the harbor fleets whose hard-working members we all catch sight of – ships, tugs, barges, ferries, fireboats, pilot boats, and police, Coast Guard, and environmental maintenance and survey vessels among them. I am in awe of their presence and the complexity of their tasks.
– *Terry Walton*

PHOTOGRAPHS, BERNARD ENTE

1

2

1 **Tug** – push or tow barges, assist vessels of all sizes
2 **Barge,** laden, unladen – carry oil, scrap steel, coal, other cargo
3 **Containership** – carry goods efficiently between world ports
4 **Ferry** – transport passengers regularly shore-to-shore within the harbor
5 **Water Taxi** – transport harbor passengers swiftly point-to-point
6 **Cruise Ship/Ocean Liner** – take passengers on recreational coastal or ocean trips
7 **Dredge** – deepen harbor or channel to accommodate ships

3

5

4

7

6

8 Drift Collection Vessel – pick up floating debris that could endanger vessel traffic or water quality

9 Fireboat – put out shore or ship fires; spray welcome on special occasions

10 Tanker – transport liquids such as oil and chemicals

11 Car Float – transport rail cars between shore connections

12 Pilot Boat – carry pilots to board and guide ships safely from sea channel through inner harbor to berth

13 Police Boat – enforce law; assist in time of trouble

14 RoRo Ship – handle roll-on, roll-off cargo such as cars, yachts, large equipment

15 Sightseeing/Excursion Vessel – take touring visitors and residents to harbor highlights or dinner cruises, oftentimes around Manhattan Island

16 Sloop, Schooner, Yawl – offer recreational or commercial harbor sails, sometimes history-themed

JOHN SENZER

8

9

10

11

★ ★ GUIDE TO HARBOR VESSELS ★ ★

*"The story of New York begins with its harbor
and the waterways that enlace the five boroughs. . . .
We invite you to explore the city's edges today – board
the working watercraft, tugs, barges, fireboats, ferries,
and others that keep the harbor working day-in, day-
out in the service of the city and its people."*

– Peter Stanford, Working Harbor Day '02,
Working Harbor Committee

14

12

15

13

16

Harbor Departings . . .
The *QE2* & Beyond

An ocean crossing had always been there, in my mind, not an active ingredient for a long time, but there. There were childhood memories of some bon voyage visits, one, I think, on the *Bremen,* in the late Thirties, something to do with Grandpa seeing off a friend. It was a late-nighter, possibly even a midnight sailing, although I can't think what [my brother] Peter and I were doing up at that hour. I remember wandering around on the promenade deck, feeling rather furtive, and discovering, parked at the very back, a seaplane. We found this to be unimaginable: a plane on a boat!

But by far the most powerful images came from the long string of sightings from shore at Rockaway Point, that slim dagger of sand pointing at the entrance to New York harbor. All of the great liners passed before us, six miles out, which somehow made them more exotic, especially as in those days they were four or five times the size of anything else afloat. They were so big they seemed like some kind of stage effect, out of proportion with everything else, like cardboard cut-outs in a kindergarten play.

"Out there was champagne and black tie; back here was beer and nine o'clock mass on Sundays."

That effect was enlarged by the publicity surrounding them. They were full of movie stars and millionaires. Here was Fred Astaire boarding the *Mauritania,* Marlene Dietrich, swathed in furs, on the *Berengaria,* people who were also six times six miles out from our lives, real but also not real. It was as though the vessels were attached to an invisible thread, just above the giant stacks, stretching its way across the sea, joining the fabled cities of the old world, London, Paris, Rome, to the New York of theatre and cafes and Park Avenue; the longitude of privilege. Out there was champagne and black tie; back here was beer and nine o'clock mass on Sundays.

Then too we had a family expert to keep our consciousness properly raised. My brother Arthur had fallen in love with liners. He read the *Times* shipping news every day. He knew the time of every arrival and departure. In those days for a quarter you could visit the

From QE2's Hudson pier . . . to Statue of liberty . . . to Verrazano-Narrows Bridge – then past Rockaway and on transatlantic.

ships when they were in port. He made a career out of it. He knew every ship's profile, the rake of the tunnels, the curve of the bow. He knew every name in every line, not just Cunard, but White Star, North German Lloyd, Hamburg-American, French. He knew all the interiors, the décor of every first-class lounge, the style of the chandeliers in the vast dining rooms. He once awakened a truly understanding neighbor at dawn to watch the *Normandie* depart.

Recently, all this was my real baggage as we tried to find our way through the maze of traffic near the pier on the appointed day for our *Queeen Elizabeth 2* sailing, my wife and I, a lifetime after those Rockaway sightings. I was about to become one of those fairy tale people. Not quite one, of course, but at least in their footsteps. It didn't matter that we had to get out of the car and roll our suitcases several blocks before we reached the ship. It didn't matter that we sailed an hour late. It didn't matter that we swung into the Hudson under an El Greco sky, coal black in parts, slate grey in others, bursts of sunlight streaming through openings that came and went, thin curtains of rain blowing in waves across us.

The shifting patterns of light and dark cast the city, slipping slowly away behind us, in a ghostly light. It didn't even matter that Rockaway Point, when the famous moment came, was no more than a few bright pinpoints in the mist. There I was, huge smokestack towering above me, an orderly line of lifeboats nestled to one side, railings all around, one deck under foot, others rising above, water everywhere, and we were moving through it, soon to be breasting the Atlantic. The ancient adventure was finally at hand. I could feel it passing through me, some long dormant need, a connection at last made, between that thin line of beach on which I was now beginning my seventy-fifth year and this grandest of her breed, the shape that had always been out on the horizon. And I was now part of that horizon.

    – David Fuchs, departing NY harbor aboard Queen Elizabeth 2, *2006*

--- ★ ---

"It was darkening when we sailed, with drinks passed on white-napkined trays for eager passengers on the afterdeck, and lights winking on in city buildings. Flags flew crisply on city buildings and on our ship. Our whistles sounded and we backed slowly out into the Hudson. The excitement was such – and silent recollections of 9/11's earlier catastrophe just downriver were so keen – that when American and British anthems were exuberantly played to honor the occasion, there were tears. . . . Nearing the Battery we saw fireworks showing over building tops – were they for us? A celebration as this glorious QM2 *departed her favorite harbor? Turns out it was something for the Brooklyn Bridge, but we knew it was really for us and* QM2.*"*

    – Terry Walton, aboard *Queen Mary 2* for Southampton, 2004

--- ★ ---

NY/NJ Cruise Ship Industry –
It's Thriving in Our Harbor

Ever since Mayor Fiorello LaGuardia blasted into bedrock to create longer passenger ship piers on Manhattan's West Side, accommodating the classic super liners along what became known as Luxury Liner Row, New York hosted transatlantic ships of the Golden Era of steamships, and continues to host cruise liners year round. While the port of NY/NJ is the third largest nationwide (LA/Long Beach are larger), with thousands of port calls annually by cargo vessels, cruise ship arrivals are for New Yorkers the most visible aspect of this largest port on the East Coast. In 2007, more than 1.5 million passengers boarded ships via the NY/NJ terminals. ★ With continuing industry growth, cruise ships of nearly every stripe parade up the North River (more familiarly the Hudson) to the Manhattan Cruise Terminal. The terminal welcomes the regulars of Carnival Cruise Lines, Norwegian Cruise Lines, Holland America Line, and others to its three piers 88-90-92 stretching from 48th to 52nd Street. Since 2006, the Brooklyn Terminal at Red Hook's Pier 12 has hosted Cunard's *Queen Mary 2* and sister cruise line Princess Cruises. Just across the river in Bayonne, Royal Caribbean and her sister lines, Celebrity Cruises and Azamara Cruises, bring ever-larger vessels into Cape Liberty Cruise Port, formerly the U.S. Army Military Ocean Terminal. Back in Manhattan, even the local Chelsea Piers get into the act with the smaller coastal ships of Clipper Cruises. ★ While newsworthy arrivals or departures of transatlantic celebrities aboard classic liners of yesteryear are eclipsed by air travel today, the cruise liner as a seagoing vacation palace has become the celebrity. The famed liner *Titanic* was 46,000 tons and the *Normandie* was the largest ship of her day at 79,000 tons – yet both would be dwarfed today by Royal Caribbean's 220,000-ton *Oasis of the Seas*. ★ Gliding into the port of New York in the early morning hours and departing in the golden sun of late afternoon, cruise vessels today, no matter size or destination, enthrall, amaze, and bring magic to passenger and shoreside spectator alike.

– *Jonathan Atkin, www.shipshooter.com*

USCG *Eagle* . . .
Harbor Recollections
From a Coast Guard Admiral

RADM Doug Teeson, USCG (Ret), tells great tales of his times aboard the Coast Guard's barque-rigged training ship *Eagle,* of Op Sail days in New York harbor, and of his years living on Governors Island just before the Coast Guard left these headquarters of long standing.

To start, Admiral Teeson recalls being aboard the *Eagle* as she was departing New York harbor just after Op Sail '64. As a Coast Guard Academy cadet, he and his classmates were on a training cruise which, earlier in the summer, had made port calls in Dublin, Ireland, and Bremen, Germany. As luck would have it, as *Eagle* cleared out of New York harbor, he was assigned to duty belowdecks in the *Eagle's* engine room. "The engine was quite a primitive affair, back then," he states. "If you didn't do things in just the right sequence when the ship was maneuvering, the engine could end up running 'inside out,' sending diesel exhaust into the engine room. We were always on our toes about that, though, and all went well on that glorious harbor day."

Many years later for Op Sail 2000 – by then he was Superintendent of the Coast Guard Academy in New London – Doug was aboard the 1,050-foot aircraft carrier *Kennedy* just off Governors Island, surrounded by the day's dignitaries and "way up in the air" on the flight deck. The Statue of Liberty and tall ships looked almost diminutive beside them, as they watched "the grand procession of ships, the harbor full of all kinds of craft, the square-rigger *Wavertree* anchored over near Governors Island, no sails set but fully rigged. . . ."

"From where we stood aboard the *Kennedy,* with the formalities of full naval review, mili-

---

★

"Many years later for Op Sail 2000 – by then he was Superintendent of the Coast Guard Academy in New London – Doug was aboard the 1,050-foot aircraft carrier Kennedy just off Governors Island, surrounded by the day's dignitaries and 'way up in the air' on the flight deck. "

★

---

tary brass, tradition, square-rigged ships and celebrations all around – from that vantage point, you could really see the city as a seaport – full of history and thriving ship business. That goes with memories from many other New York harbor experiences – including even more recently, sailing down the Hudson on the *QM2* at night. What a magnificent harbor it is!"

RADM Teeson . . . USCG training ship Eagle, *as sketched by Op Sail founder Frank Braynard.*

Admiral Teeson is no stranger to the *Eagle* crew's work on those Op Sail days. Recalling a transatlantic trip to Scotland, as a junior cadet in 1962: "It seemed at first like a lot of make-work – brass to be polished, decks to be scrubbed, then suddenly the call 'all hands to sail stations,' and up in the rig we went. We were on our way to Edinburgh, sailing across the top of Scotland to enter the North Sea, and got caught aback with all sails set. My normal sail station was up on the royal yard, but on this occasion I found myself out on the main yard on the Flemish horse, with a very exuberant senior cadet beside me shouting "Use both hands! Use both hands!" He was jumping up and down on the footrope, the sail still bellying out below us as if to pry our toes off the footrope, and it was very hard to get a fistful of canvas. I thought sure I would end up taking a swim . . . it's times like that you find physical reserves that you didn't know you had. Which is one part of what *Eagle* is all about."

It was on later *Eagle* trips and visits, Doug recalls, that "I came to understand *Eagle* for what she really is – a leadership lab, a teamwork trainer. Maybe some cadets can see it that way right away, but for me the recognition came later. Standing on the quarterdeck during a sail evolution, it's like a ballet. You see who handles shared tasks well . . . who are the natural leaders, who are the developing ones, and once in a while one who just isn't getting it at all."

Doug's favorite place in New York harbor? It is Governors Island, where he and his family lived for three years just before USCG headquarters there were closed down in 1996. He was a flag officer by then, and his command oversaw or carried out most of the numerous moves – to Fort Wadsworth on Staten Island, and to Norfolk, Portsmouth, Charleston, and elsewhere. It went remarkably smoothly despite lots of island-to-off-island complexities – including the need for the moving vans to show up when the tide was right for them to get on and off the ferries. "This whole evolution was a shining example of the dedication of Coast Guard people, including many lifelong Brooklynites, who made the move to Norfolk and other places with their jobs."

Today Doug Teeson is the head of Connecticut's famous Mystic Seaport, but his NY harbor loyalties remain strong. "My hope is that Governors Island will be restored to life, a life that involves a learning environment, and that the island's history be preserved and that more of the public can experience the magic of being there," he says. "I remember when my wife and I used to go out for a walk every evening, going over first to the Buttermilk Channel side, and from there clockwise around the island. We never tired of it – the sunsets behind the Statue of Liberty, the city lights at night, the hustle-bustle of the harbor shipping. It was very moving. And we'd think, just seven minutes away by boat, there's the greatest city in the world."

– *Terry Walton*

New York's 15th Annual Tugboat Race & Competition

For the past fifteen years, on the Sunday before Labor Day, an unusual event has taken place in the North (aka Hudson) River properly called The Great North River Tugboat Race & Competition. For its first twelve years it was hosted and produced by the Intrepid Sea*Air*Space Museum and was headed by Capt. Jerry Roberts, the event's founder, with tug industry leaders. Most recently it has been hosted by the Working Harbor Committee, for the 15th anniversary year in 2007. The 16th race date . . . August 31, 2008.

For 2007 the event took place at Pier 84 in Hudson River Park, just one block south of its original location, with Jerry active as the chief judge and announcer. The spectacular race and competition drew tugs of all kinds and sizes – from the 7,000 hp *Lincoln Sea*, race winner overall in 2006, to the tiny historic *W.O. Decker* from South Street Seaport Museum, a perennial winner of the Little Toot Award. Winner for 2007's 15th annual event – in which no fewer than nineteen tugs participated – was *Lucy Reinauer* of Reinauer Transportation. The first six tugs finished within ten seconds of each other.

The competition begins with tugs parading upriver, accompanied by fireboats spraying water and by a sleek USCG cutter, followed by the one-nautical-mile race itself, with awards in several horsepower categories. The sight of a dozen or more powerful tugs racing at full throttle down the river is nothing less than awesome.

Following the race, two other competitions provide in-water action. One, the "nose-to-nose" pushing contests occur as one tug challenges another, and both tugs face off bow-to-bow as each attempts to push the other backwards. Sometime the results can be surprising! The other is the line toss, where tugs approach the pier and are timed as they attempt to

---
★

"Yes, we come out for the Tug Race every year and we like to have the public watch, to learn something about the industry. We're a small community, tugs, and we get to know everyone in it. My wife Juliette and three sons Stephen, Astin, and Zachary all have tugs named after them."

– Chris Reinauer, Reinauer Transportation

★

"lasso" a bollard without touching the pier. It's a contest that involves a high degree of coordination and precision between the captain and the line handler. In 2006 the winner was *Janice Ann Reinauer;* for 2007 it was tug *Robert IV* of Henry Marine.

Afterwards the tugs all tie up at the pier and the awards ceremony takes place – with additional winners in such categories as Best Dressed Crew, Best Looking Tug, Best Crew Member Tattoo, Best Tugboat Mascot, and Best Historic Tug. It's a competition, yes, but it's also a way for tugs crews to let off steam and have fun – a welcome respite from the serious

Tugs churning down-Hudson to the finish line . . . line toss to pier-edge bollard . . . bow-to-bow pushing contest.

"For tugs, every day is busy . . ."

"Every day is busy, there's no other way. The companies are growing, building new vessels to phase out the single hull barges for double hull, for carrying petroleum products. The last new tug project was the Meredith C. Reinauer, *launched in '04 and named for my first cousin Bert's daughter. We've been in the tug business for eighty years, working in New York harbor and going up and down the East Coast, Maine to Florida. Dad used to take us fishing on the* Janice Reinauer *when we were kids. . . ."*

– Chris Reinauer, Reinauer Transportation

On Tug Race day, bagpiper in parade . . . later, visitors welcome.

and often dangerous work of harbor and offshore towing. And it's a way to remind the public of this work: these vessels and crews do their critical tasks 24/7, seven days a week, year in and out in all weathers and seasons.

As the day winds down, the refreshed crews make their way back aboard their respective powerful water-borne workhorses, and depart to go back to work, already thinking ahead to next year. . . .

– *Capt. John Doswell, Working Harbor Committee*

Geo Matteson's Book
Tugboats of New York

It was not only the deep-sea class of mariners who captured the popular imagination. Another, homegrown type of vessel, the tugboat, worked its way into the awareness of the people.

During that time, tugs established themselves as an essential part of the well-being and efficiency of the port. They assumed the duty of transporting vast quantities of produce, goods, and raw materials. They developed the capacity not only to nudge ships to and from their berths alongshore but also to range far out to sea in all sorts of weather to find and assist

ships as they approached the harbor. The tugs toughened and grew in endurance enough to tow across oceans. They facilitated a succession of new industries such as the railroads and the broad-scale transport of coal and, later, of industrial chemicals and oil.

Although every seaport in America has tugboats, their history is revealed most completely in New York. Most of the crucial development of the trade took place in New York, and that is certainly where all those developments, wherever they first arose, have been thoroughly tested.

Today, much of the activity of the harbor has shifted away from the metropolis to the great shipping terminals of Ports Newark and Elizabeth. The number of tugs has diminished along with the Port of New York's position of East Coast and national dominance. But still, a glimpse of the water from any point in the city may include a passing tugboat; and any misty night may carry the sound of a tug's horn far up into the streets. They are still with us, and so is their story.

★ ★ ★

We were southbound in the Hudson, just coming out of the gutter above Saugerties and riding the freshet. We had left the canal just a little after midnight, running light back to New York after dropping off a contractor's barge just east of Little Falls. I had been steering since daylight. My relief and the deckhand were asleep below. It had been five days since we had started on this job, and we were all tired. It was a bright sunny morning in early spring. The maples on the hillsides were showing no green as yet – only the deep-red haze of quickening buds and twigs. In the settlements along shore it was still the season of blue tarps. . . .

Downstream at the bottom of the next reach was a big northbound tug pushing a loaded oil barge. It labored upriver against the current and the backdrop of its own black smoke. The sun glanced off the flat face of the tug's radar antenna each time it completed a rotation, and the vessel thus appeared to possess a tiny heartbeat. Normally there would be no need for communication between a light tug and a tow meeting in broad daylight on an open stretch of river. By custom the light tug is entrusted to stay clear of the other, a professional courtesy. But this morning the captain of the northbound tug called me in a gravelly Southern voice.

He had a deckhand on board who had to get home for a medical emergency. Did I know someplace downriver where he could catch a train? Would I take him there? . . .

– *George Matteson*, Tugboats of New York, *2005*

———— ★ ————

"New York Harbor is a confluence of stone and silts, waters fresh and salt, varied peoples and ideas, infinite constructions and the raw materials necessary to them."
– George Matteson, *Tugboats of New York*

———— ★ ————

NOTE – *The deckhand transfer was done and the train caught, with a wave from train engineer to tug captain Geo Matteson. Geo's* Tugboats of New York *(New York University Press, 2005) reflects his decades of experience and research and his remarkable storytelling skills. When Capt. Brian McAllister introduced Geo at a recent Working Harbor Committee awards dinner, and spoke of his book and its remarks by tugmen, he said, "Reading this book is like listening to my grandfather speak to me." At which point Capt. McAllister had to stop talking a moment to regain his composure. This is a splendid book! TW*

Containerships – Where Do Your Sneakers Come From & How Do They Get Here?

A little over a half century ago, a ship called the *Ideal X* departed from Pier 26 in Port Newark, New Jersey, and changed ocean-going shipping–and along with it, the global economy – forever. The *Ideal X,* the world's first container ship, carried fifty-eight truck trailers, filled with cargo, lashed to her deck. They weren't actually complete trailers: they were steel boxes, without tires or running gear. When the vessel reached her destination, in Houston, the trailers were lifted onto wheeled chassis and trucked to their destinations where the cargo was unloaded. A new era in shipping that promised cheaper, safer, and faster commerce of all sorts of commodities around the world had arrived.

Fast forward to today's global economy with a vital lifeline of 200 million containers shipped annually around the world, in which the Port Newark–Elizabeth Marine Terminal serves as the primary container ship facility for the metropolitan region of New York City and the northeastern quadrant of North America. It's a long way from the day of sail when clipper ships bearing goods from the Far East docked at the South Street piers of Manhattan after months-long voyages. Now, the ships are called container ships, and they can haul thousands of twenty- and forty-foot steel boxes stacked in the ship's hold and on its decks.

What's inside all of those containers? Essentially, just about anything you can imagine: fresh fruit and vegetables (in refrigerated containers); electronics, including computers, TVs, and cell phones; household goods like mops, brooms, and dustpans; sheets and linens; clothing and shoes. Take your sneakers, for example. That pair of Reeboks is packed, along with thousands of other pairs of sneakers and other goods for export, into a container parked at a loading dock at a factory outside of Shanghai. After the doors of the forty-foot steel container are closed, a worker seals them shut with a steel bolt with an ID code stamped on it. (The bolt ensures that the container's contents will not be pilfered or tampered with. It will not be removed until the container checks in at its final destination.)

Next, a truck hauls the container to Shanghai's container port, where it is loaded onto a container ship with hundreds of other similar containers. The ship crosses the Pacific, transits the Panama Canal and heads up the East Coast of the United States. It might stop at other container ports along the way – Savannah, Charleston, Norfolk – before it reaches the Port Newark–Elizabeth Marine Terminal in Newark Bay. There, using gigantic lifting cranes that tower nearly 400 feet tall and can reach 200 feet over a container ship's deck and the dock's strange looking wheeled devices called "straddle carriers," the container is unloaded from the ship and trucked to its final destination – Reebok's distribution center in the northeastern United States. From there, it's trucked to your local Reebok store.

The container itself – with its contents – is tracked start-to-finish throughout its travels, so that when it arrives at its destination, shipping agents and U.S. Customs know exactly where the container is from and what it holds. That's essential, because the scene at the container port is breathtaking in size and scale, and without computers, finding a single container in a storage yard filled with thousands of them could be likened to finding the proverbial needle in a haystack.

Steven Bendo (r) with James McGeehan at Port Elizabeth.

The Port Newark–Elizabeth Marine Terminal is the largest container port in the eastern United States and the second largest in the country. Only Los Angeles–Long Beach in California is larger. It consists of two components – Port Newark and the Elizabeth Marine Terminal, sometimes called "Port Elizabeth," which are located side by side and are run by the Port Authority of New York and New Jersey. Both were planned and built during the 1950s by the Port Authority; containers typically arrive on ships through the lower harbor's Verrazano Narrows and then the Kill Van Kull, which separates Staten Island from Bayonne, New Jersey. The facility consists of two main dredged ship channels a mile and a half long and thousands of acres of storage yards and facilities for trucks and rail cars. Incoming and outgoing steel containers are stacked up to three high in vast holding areas that are visible from the New Jersey Turnpike before they are loaded onto trucks or trains. Today the port operators include Maher Terminals, APM Terminal (Maersk), Port Newark Container Terminal, New York Container Terminal, Global Marine Terminal, and American Stevedoring.

One of the key people who keep it all running smoothly is James McGeehan, Director Administration & Depots for Maher Terminals. Jim has worked in shipping for twenty-six years, but before that he was a schoolteacher. His teaching experience shows in his excellent

Containers coming in by truck are checked via remote work stations manned by ILA checkers, using the latest OCR camera technology. Vessels at Port Elizabeth await loading or unloading by cranes – with their containers meticulously arranged on ship or pier depending on weight, content, destination, and other factors, and are helped in docking and undocking by skilled and trusty tugs.

JIM TOURTELOTTE FOR CUSTOMS AND BORDER PATROL

Did you know? . . . a book edited in NY and printed in Hong Kong - after many Internet and air-freight proofings - left Hong Kong by container-ship on 4/14/08 via Pacific Ocean and Panama Canal, reaching NY harbor on 5/7/08 for shipping out via truck or train.

Straddle carriers (top right) position containers precisely for lifting and loading by crane. Ashore on the pier, all incoming receive diverse inspections, then depart inland via truck or train for destinations local or long distance. Containers are numbered on all sides for ease in tracking throughout land and transoceanic journeys.

running commentary on the workings of the port as he drives a company minibus through Maher's 463-acre terminal. (No private vehicles are permitted in the facility for reasons that are obvious when you are confronted with the scale of the place.)

"There's one of our straddle carriers," he says as the ungainly upside-down U-shaped wheeled contraption disappears down a row of stacked 40-foot containers. "The operator is in a cab forty feet above the ground," Jim explains, " because he sits above the containers below that can be stacked three high." Actually, the term "straddle carrier" perfectly describes the machine's function: It straddles the container and lifts it off the ground using the four twist-locks in each of a container's four corners.

"The straddle carrier operators work in teams of three using two carriers, so that one of the three operators is on break while the other two are in constant motion," says Jim. "A computer mounted on his dashboard tells the operator where to find the correct container. He always tries to do a double move: He delivers an import container and picks up another container for export." Straddle carriers are very expensive and Maher's fleet of 183 machines – the largest fleet in the U.S. – represents a significant investment.

Next, we head to the end of Maher's terminal area where wharfs that are currently being expanded front directly on Newark Bay. Here are the gigantic lifting cranes – Super Post Panamax Gantry Cranes – that can lift sixty-five-ton containers a hundred twenty feet in the air across a two-hundred-foot-wide container ship deck, or twenty-two containers across. "The cranes are state of the art and the biggest and best cranes available," says Jim. "They're electrically powered, with a cable that unwinds from a giant spool and runs under a rubber flap to protect the cable from damage. The crane operators, International Longshoremen's Association members, are the most important labor personnel hired on the terminal. Their skill and expertise allows us to produce almost twenty-nine crane moves per crane per hour, allowing us to turn vessels timely and productively."

When a ship arrives in port with thousands of containers for unloading, the operation is choreographed by computer: Straddle carriers remove and deliver the containers in precise order, with three to five cranes and dozens of straddle carriers working each ship. "We get, on average, twenty-six container ships a week," says Jim. "Of those twelve or thirteen are from the Far East – China, Japan, Hong Kong, and Indonesia. The rest are from Northern Europe, Africa, the Mediterranean, and South America.

One of several people that Jim works with in the intricate planning needed for all this is Steven Bendo, an experienced ex chief mate now land-based to do this extraordinarily complex job. Bendo understands exactly what's required to plan the vessel's loading in the most efficient way possible, and arranges for it to be so (see Harbor Jobs & Waterfront Explorations, page 23).

Maher handles 1.25 million containers a year, most of them delivered within a fifty-mile radius of the port. Also 7,000 containers a week are double-stacked on rail cars and hauled to the Midwest and to Montreal (sending them by "steel wheels" instead of "rubber tires," in the lingo of the port). Some 5,000 trucks a day transit Maher's Fleet Street Terminal daily ("a trucker can do six to eight containers a day if he hustles," says Jim) – a facility that has enough truck lanes to handle twice that number. As each truck enters the lane complex with its steel box, digital cameras snap twenty-six photos from all angles. That allows Maher's truck processing clerks and TIR men to inspect and process all exports and empties and assign them to their proper location. Every import container also gets a radiation check, a Customs-required process installed to meet the demands of Homeland Security. Containers are also singled out and given thorough checks for drugs and contraband by Customs agents, using a manifest review system which allows for random exams along with CET and MET team exams.

"When a ship arrives in port with thousands of containers for unloading, the operation is choreographed by computer: Straddle carriers remove and deliver the containers in precise order . . ."

The building of the Port Newark–Elizabeth Marine Terminal container port facility made many of the existing waterfront facilities in New York Harbor obsolete overnight, leading to a sharp decrease in waterfront cargo handling in areas such as Manhattan, Hoboken, and Brooklyn. The container port is itself booming, however. Since 1998, the port overall has had a 65 percent increase in cargo volume. In 2003 the port handled more than $100 billion in goods, and plans are underway for billions of dollars in improvements – more and larger lifting cranes, expanded railroad facilities, and deeper and longer wharves – and new longshoremen are being hired as well. Today, nearly four hundred years after it was discovered, the Port of New York still serves as a vital link in global commerce.

– *Richard Stepler*

One major container terminal in Port Elizabeth, NJ, sends about 26 ships a week to the Far East (China, Japan, Hong Kong, other), South America, or South Africa.

★

The Panama Canal (connects Atlantic and Pacific oceans via Central America) has size restrictions, so as ships get bigger, the Suez Canal (connects Mediterranean and Red Sea in Egypt) is used increasingly – thus revolutionizing certain major shipping routes. A new set of Panama Canal locks is scheduled for completion in 2015 to accommodate larger vessels.

★

One NJ port facility handles 5,000 trucks a day at a 24-hour gate, with 6 a.m. to midnight extended hours for loading/offloading trucked containers. Equals 1.3 million containers per year.

★

Containers are generally 20-footers or 40-footers, made of strong corrugated steel with twist-lock holes in 4 corners for secure lifting by crane or straddle carrier, and secure fastening to truck body or rail car. Any container's key numbers appear on all surfaces to be read by crane operators, cameras, customs officials, other checkers.

★

For every container, computers are used to determine the best booking slot on land or aboard ship, considering weight, contents, destination, safety, other loading/storing factors – all overseen by port personnel.

★

Train tracks run right through port facilities, bringing in containers from across the country; current port facility goal to ease upland traffic: more trains, fewer trucks.

★

A RoRo (roll on, roll off) carrier can have 13 decks on which to handle cars shipped from overseas.

Places – Up the Creeks & Behind the Scenes

Well, the 1970s-'90s "Places" articles are really all the fault of my co-worker Norman Brouwer. As librarian and ship historian for South Street Seaport Museum and the World Ship Trust, and as Robert Albion's successor in recording the history of the port of New York, he knew all the best places for exploration. Among them, Port Johnston, the graveyard off Staten Island where graceful old sailing ships lay as their timbers disintegrated over time . . . nearby Shooter's Island with its egret rookery and vestiges of World War II shipyard buildings . . . Battery Weed, that grand stone post-Revolutionary structure at Fort Wadsworth and the Verrazano Bridge. Ashore, of course, I was fortunate in South Street's proximity to the Jasper Ward house (its tin ceiling elegant still) . . . the Fulton Market (recorded so strikingly in Naima Rauam's paintings) . . . and of course rowdy Carmine's Bar, one block from our offices and the perfect place for cold beers at the end of the day. ★ More recently have come return visits to the beautiful arch-windowed brick warehouses called Empire Stores, north of the Brooklyn Bridge, and lining Atlantic and Erie basins further south . . . and to the tug yards and Noble Maritime Collection exhibits along Staten Island's Kill Van Kull, and on under the graceful arch of the Bayonne Bridge. So many hidden things and so much exploring still to do. . . . *TW*

Fish Market fish – the freshest. Time was they came in by schooner or other fisherman's vessel to South Street, in the Museum's earliest days, in vessels with great names: Lady of Good Voyage, Two Brothers, Felicia, Lady of Fatima, *and* Victor *were among them. . . . Shad man slits female, removes roe, and flips fish onto scale or into bins, sorting by size. Behind him wholesalers' offices and stall numbers are named – "5, Lockwin & Co." as here, or "19, R. J. Cornelius & Co." Wholesalers numbered 80–100 in the 1970s.*

Fulton Fish Market . . .
Spending the Night With City & Sea

TODAY – The Fulton Fish Market (1973) moved to the Bronx in 2005, but people still tell Market stories in South Street.

Sadly for all New Yorkers, "progress" edges the Fulton Fish Market toward a new site at Hunt's Point. But its history is a South Street legend now, and a night in the Market is still without equal.

Midnight in April and the first big trailer trucks come in – Tidewater Express from Crisfield, Maryland, then Axelsson & Johnson Fish Co. from Cape May. Unloaders open the truck backs and haul out crates, five to a handcart, to be wheeled to where the wholesaler's journeyman points. Shouts mount and fish come in, not aboard South Street's beamy smacks as they once did, during the last century, but now in fancy refrigerated diesel vans that head for Fulton Fish Market from every East Coast state and from ships from South America and Africa – because demand and money are good here.

⭐

"Fearless journeymen maneuver their crates between two trucks inching by each other. Some tempers are short by now ('Get him out of there! Go round the back!') . . ."

⭐

Once caught, iced, crated, and trucked to their Market stacks by about 2 a.m. the fish await smaller panel trucks – perhaps from Popular Fish Market or Joe's Clam Bar, filling an order of clams or lobsters or reds and blues. Or the fish are persuasively hawked ("I can get you good porgy and whiting – over here, take a look!" . . .), or displayed by size in the wholesaler's bin, large shad here, medium there, small over here, freshly excised roe neatly slung into foot-square pans.

By four a.m. the last of the big trucks are being unloaded while others are snarled in traffic at Fulton and South, trying to come and go but accomplishing neither. Fearless journeymen maneuver their crates between two trucks inching by each other. Some tempers are short by now ("Get him out of there! Go round the back!"), and the few unfilled orders are being discovered and sworn at. Unloaders may take a break to go for coffee at Carmine's at Beekman and Front.

First light softly illumines the Brooklyn Bridge by five or six. Traffic is tight still. A chef himself selects the fish that maintains his reputation. Empty crates accumulate; some men burn a few to drive away the chill. Clean-up begins.

Down at Meyer's Hotel or the John St. Diner over scrambled and extra bacon the totals are added and compared ("How much was he asking for the blues?" or "I'll never do that again – I figured 15 cents apiece you'd make something, but I filleted them and there's no meat on 'em").

Brothers, uncles, fathers, and sons in Vinny Lategano's unloading crew briefly discuss the work completed. Samuel Titen (L. Grand Cutlery and Scales, scales, knives, gloves, hooks, corner of Beekman and South) prepares to close for the day. And everywhere is the sweet pungence of fish, hardly noticed anymore by Fish Market men, extolled by noon visitors to the Seaport or Sweet's or Sloppy Louie's, never fully erased by even the heaviest rains.

And by now bosses, wholesalers, journeymen, unloaders, and truckers are getting ready for the rest, well earned, until all the healthy bedlam begins again that night, while New York sleeps.

– *Terry Walton, South Street Reporter 1973,
South Street Seaport Museum*

The square-backed trucks of a century ago are gone, but the Peck Slip buildings shown here still stand, many restored to glory.

★ *Changes with time – As long envisioned, the Fulton Fish Market left South Street in 2005 – relocated to modern quarters in the Bronx – and with it went the reek of fish that some loved and others hated. Remaining, however, are architectural features such as the wriggly fish tie-rod ends on 142 Beekman Street, extraordinary Market paintings by artist Naima Rauam, and the century-old Fish Market bar called Carmine's, lively as ever at the Beekman-Front Street intersection. TW*

The Jasper Ward House – Elegance in Pressed Tin

This piece of the pressed tin ceiling of the Jasper Ward House, 45 Peck Slip down near the Brooklyn Bridge and Fulton Market, was propped up on the sidewalk one afternoon in 1979, part of a Columbia University/South Street preservation project. It was noted one day, by happenstance, by professional photographer Jeff Perkell, who said "Yes!" to a request to feature it in Seaport *magazine.* – Seaport Magazine 1979, South Street Seaport Museum

SEA FOOD CARMINE'S · BAR · GRILL

CARMINE'S BAR AND GRILL SEA FOOD   CARMINE'S

97 - 43 M

Carmine's today (above) in evocative painting by local artist Naima Rauam. . . . "Carmine's Bar and Grill," as shown in a 1940 New York Tax Department photograph – during the "Fish Market Bar" era.

112

Carmine's Bar . . .
Red Sauce Italian Fish House

Want a side order of Fulton Fish Market history with your calamari marinara? Over the past 100 years, the mahogany bar and the oak-paneled walls at Carmine's Italian Seafood Restaurant in the heart of the South Street Seaport have seen a thing or two.

If old downtown bars could only talk. Superficially, the dark mahogany bar at Carmine's, perfect elbow height for thirsty customers perched on barstools, heels slung on the brass foot-rail below. Ask Greg Molini, manager of ninety-nine-year-old Carmine's Italian Seafood Restaurant, a.k.a. Carmine's Bar. It's on Beekman Street, amidst the scenes and scents of the Fulton Fish Market. Greg knows lots of boisterous stories told over time at the bar.

Celebrating its centennial in 2003, Carmine's is a direct connection to another time – of fishing smacks docked at the foot of the street, of the midnight shouts of Fish Market men selling their wares, of a quieting down at dawn, of trudging to local eateries in the first light of morning for spaghetti and wine when the night's work is over. With famous old Sloppy Louie's and Sweet's restaurants both gone, the Paris Cafe and McCormack's (today the Bridge Cafe) are, with Carmine's, the sole survivors of that rowdy earlier South Street time.

Carmine's exterior is peeling blue-green paint with a ship's-wheel sign angled out over the street. The honorably shabby building, traditional red brick above with a rusticated white block facade below, is historic in itself. A 1968 Landmark Preservation Commission inventory reveals that 140 Beekman Street was built for Joseph and Elias Drake in 1824, at the height of South Street's bustling city market and square-rigger years. The 1824 building replaced a prior one on the site the same year Beekman Street was widened, a busy two-block-long street that led straight to the ships and piers.

City directories of those years show Elias G. Drake as a merchant and Joseph as a grocer, both living in houses nearby. Carmine's corner door once opened on Front Street, hence its 212 Front Street alias in city surveys. Its broad, arch-topped windows are typical of storefronts in the 1820s.

Carmine's Bar thus documents the district's historic connection with East River ships and markets – meat, fish, and produce among them. It also gives visual contrast to the upscale

Seaport shops across the street, which glisten in green and glass.

"Give me spaghetti *alio olio* and another round of Bass Ale," says Julio, one of Greg's long-time waiters. "Then two scungilli salads, two softshells and a calamari marinara." It's for a row of tables near the door, dark-varnished like the bar and full of stories too, small tables easily pushed together or apart as needed, and bordered by booths likewise dark and glistening. At the Bass Ale table, old friends lean in toward each other, elbows a fulcrum for the beers, all talking at once about a harbor event. They've been customers for years.

It's 5 o'clock and still pretty quiet. The chairs are back on the floor after the daily post-lunch scrub-down. The after-work regulars will show up soon. They're a mixed lot: lawyers; stock brokers; shippers; skippers of tugs, fireboats, sloops and schooners; as well as rising yuppies on to a cool place for dinner and full of the day.

Dawn and morning hours are no longer needed here by the Fish Market men. These days, Carmine's opens for lunch for the locals, walkovers from Wall Street and adventurers down from uptown. But now it's time for evening's rowdy crowd. Noise picks up, beer flows, garlic bread appears on tables and chilled-glass gimlets at the bar, prepared by bartender Bobby Bond. Familiar faces keep coming in. By 7 there isn't a seat left. Greg's visiting a table or two.

Newcomers, seated and orders placed, look around and wonder about the wooden half-hull ship models and the fish plaques on the walls. "They've just always been here," Greg says. He points out the globe lights on the dark wood and cane ceiling fans and the original pressed-tin ceiling, its sections framed by old moldings and beams. The walls are history in themselves: dark oak tongue-and-groove paneling that has seen a thing or two.

Greg leans a shoulder against the wall at the end of the bar. He's talking on the pay phone as he greets customers with a wave. This man loves telling stories, and he's proud of Carmine's near and distant past, some of it catastrophic with floods and blackouts, some of it colorful with famous patrons: Chuck Connor, Alan Alda, and Mayor Ed Koch among them.

Greg's first memories of Carmine's are from age twelve when he came with his father Vincent and stepmother Piera to see the family's newly purchased restaurant. It was in 1977, he recalls, and the restaurant was closed weekends. Back then it was mostly Fish Market clientele and still in the early years of the South Street Seaport Museum. "It was small and manageable, and we fell in love with it," says Vincent. "My wife was a waitress and I sold office equipment and knew the area. We both loved to cook and loved to eat, so we took a shot."

"We took everything out on the sidewalk and washed it down," says Greg. "Then we did the same inside: the walls, the floors, the kitchen, all of it. We even sponge-mopped the ceiling. Did you ever hear of anyone doing that?" He also remembers thinking, "This is a happy day. My dad has a restaurant and that means I can eat for free, as much as I want."

Greg mentions an old copy of *Reader's Digest*, recounting the 1979-81 Fulton Market investigations by the U.S. Attorney's Office, with some market men going to jail for extortion and more. "The Fish Market Union is still a tenant here, right upstairs," Greg points up over his head. "I've got that *Digest* article here somewhere; want to see it?" "Loan sharks, bookmakers, and extortionists were as numerous as the fish," the article says of the Fish Market in the 1920s.

Carmine Russo, the original owner and namesake of Carmine's Bar, was also listed as the Fish Market Union's business representative in the 1970s. When did Carmine open his restaurant? "Since 1903," reads the restaurant slogan today. To hear Greg tell it, the date has a whimsical origin. . . .

"Years ago an old woman came in and out of the blue started telling me some stories, so I just shut up and listened." From this talkative woman, and from Carmine Russo himself, Greg and his father have put the story together. During Prohibition in the 1920s, 140 Beekman Street had a speakeasy upstairs, and before that, at the turn of the century in the market's heyday, it was an eatery downstairs selling a bit of liquor on the side. Carmine himself, it is said, began his restaurant career as a boy, selling food from a milk crate on the corner of Beekman Street and later in the Fulton Market building itself.

"So my father, a bit of a storyteller himself," Greg says, "simply included the eatery's early years and honored his mother in the bargain. 'Let's make 1903 the starting date,' he said. 'That's the year my mother was born.'" Hence, the 2003 centennial.

In those years at the turn of the century, big ice trucks jammed the streets from midnight on, replacing the horse-drawn wagons of earlier times. Fish came ashore from schooners at the river's edge, crated and carted from pier to street to market. The deep rumble of hand trucks

---
★

"In those years at the turn of the century, big ice trucks jammed the streets from midnight on, replacing the horse-drawn wagons of earlier times. Fish came ashore from schooners at the river's edge, crated and carted from pier to street to market. . . ."

★
---

and wheelbarrows on Belgian block paving, the night-long shouts of sellers and buyers, and the haste for the finest and quickest deals were surely cacophonous, just as they still were in the 1970s in the Seaport Museum's founding years.

Photographs confirm the chock-a-block crowded ways of the old market and the stacks of barrels, pallets, and sacks lining the streets in both horse- and gasoline-powered eras. Come dawn, the wagons and trucks would head out for their deliveries, fish stalls got their final hosing down, and all that was left was fish scales in the streets and the pungent scents of the night's work. It was at 5 a.m. or so that the coffee-and-rolls offerings of the midnight before became morning's pasta, eggs, fish, wine, the works for the market men. At Carmine's and the other eateries around, it was dinner at dawn.

Carmine Russo himself – who operated his restaurant from the mid-1930s before selling it to Vincent Molini in 1977 – was a colorful local figure. Friends enjoy telling some oft-repeated stories. Among them, Greg recalls hearing, is that each wholesaler respectfully offered Carmine a choice fish or two each day, so that by morning's end he had a fresh supply for his customers.

Former Carmine's waitress Marie Colletti retired after twelve years of a Staten Island-to-Manhattan commute. Her time overlapped Carmine Russo's ownership by a couple of years.

"He was big, tall, and well-built, muscular, grey-haired by then. He took no nonsense from anyone. He liked me, and when Carmine liked you, you were his friend." Marie recalls that Carmine Russo loved his work. "The restaurant was his whole life: He'd be up all night for the market, then almost asleep at the booth by morning, hand on knee and knee up against the table. It was always the third booth back. Then someone would drive him home."

Marie also remembers Carmine's gravelly deep voice and that he liked everyone to think he was tough and frugal. "But then he'd turn around and say, in his low can't-be-overheard voice, 'Marie, here's $10, don't tell anyone!' Or it would be $20, and it would be for any of us who had been out sick, or who had lots of children, or some kind of problem. We were like a family . . . we had respect for each other, asked after each other. Birthday cakes – usually I'd bake them."

Carmine Russo died in the winter of 1982. Marie knows the exact date of the wake from her Mass card, one of many she keeps from those days. And she still has the last $10 Carmine gave her.

Greg and his wife Cinzia, who took over management from Vincent in 1983, know much about the history of the Seaport and their restaurant's role in it. Greg remembers the lesser floods when seawater seeped in merely ankle deep, with patrons enjoying lunch as usual while the staff push-broomed the water back out the door. He remembers city blackouts and the loss of all the food in the place, shocking financial hits that were hard to get through, and the whole staff coming in the next day to throw things out, to bleach and clean every inch to get the place ready for operation the minute power was restored.

He also remembers the big flood – wintry winds with surging East River tide one morning in 1992. He got a call from Manuel, the chef. River water was two feet deep on Beekman Street and rising.

Greg got there fast, and by then the tabletops were nearly underwater. He sloshed across the booth tops to reach the kitchen gas shutoff, his head and hands well submerged once he finally found the right place. And he remembers feeling sad at the mess of it all, and cold, and trying to get warm afterwards with a hit of blackberry brandy he found on a shelf. "I felt like crying," he says. "All that saltwater eating away at the restaurant."

Greg counted blessings that no one was hurt, closed the shutters, locked up and sent everyone home. Then he went off to borrow a truck. He rented a generator and found a powerful pump somewhere. And again, all hands rallied in the ensuing days. Carmine's was back in business in less than a week.

"Carmine's has the tables at which these stories are told."

– New York Harbor historian Conrad Milster, telling maritime stories in the engine room of the coal-burning ferry *Weehawken*

"You see, it's the staff," Greg says of his place. "We have waiters and waitresses alternating their hours, plus bartenders, cooks, dishwashers and a busboy. Bobby, Julio, Irene, Baboo, Manuel, Bolivar, Jose: They all fit in here. Take Julio: He's been here the longest. . . ."

Silver-haired and handsome Julio lives in New Jersey and has been a Carmine's waiter for seventeen years. Julio has a heartwarming smile and his own following at Carmine's, and he likes to mention that coming anniversary year. He's from Argentina and is proud of the success of his three sons, today well along in careers in computers and on Wall Street.

Julio has seen his share of distinguished guests for dinner. He remembers the time the

U.S. Open was in town and some famous players came to Carmine's. It seems a big platter of fish slid into someone's lap. There was, fortunately, laughter all around. Of his career at Carmine's Julio says, in his quiet voice, "It's a nice place. I have good friends here."

"My years at Carmine's were good," adds Marie Colletti. "A completely good experience for me both before Greg and after he came. I was afraid of change, but it was a good change, and we were very close-knit. I always felt at home." She remembers the flood times, too. "Customers would just sit there and keep on eating as the water seeped under the door." She'd simply put on boots and keep working.

Of Vincent she says, "I remember him coming into the place a couple of times before he bought it. He was a gentleman, hardworking, and he made good changes." Asked whether she'd made suggestions to eighteen-year-old Greg when he took over, Marie smiles. "Oh, no, his stepmother Piera did that. He was so young and I was so old!"

One regular Carmine's visitor these days is Vincent Molini himself. Vincent stays in touch with the restaurant's finances and other comings and goings. He is a dapper dresser with a mustache and graying hair, and he looks younger than you'd expect. Vincent received his degree in history eight years ago and now teaches at Mercy College, upstate near Peekskill, and volunteers at a drug rehabilitation center near his home.

Vincent remembers the lumbering reefer trucks filling the streets, the 11 p.m. rolls and coffee and the 5 a.m. spaghetti and wine before he made the transition from fish market hours (all night and all mornings, no lunch, no weekends) to today's regular restaurant hours as the Seaport grew and market activities waned. He remembers Mayor Koch's habitual lunchtime visits and favorite half-and-half order of calamari marinara and scungilli with nothing to drink. Matt Dillon, Frank Gifford, and Sterling Hayden are among other well-known names from Vincent's years. Not to mention the South Street Seaport Museum people, including tugboat owner Geo Matteson, whose uncle's schooner *Pioneer* is today part of the Seaport fleet, and the revered old merchant mariner and poet, the late Ed Moran.

Today, one of Greg's recent memories has to do with the events of September 11, 2001, when everyone around South Street came together to help.

"I was on the Verrazano Bridge and saw the smoke," he says. "I called my wife. Manuel and Jose, our chefs, were at work and waited there. I got to Carmine's somehow, and we set up a kind of depot, getting our food over to St. Paul's Chapel, and then ice – I had the key to my friend Tommy's ice company in the market. I knew he wouldn't mind. So we took tons and tons of it over to keep the food fresh."

That morning Greg and others put yellow duct tape in the shape of a cross on three SUVs going back and forth between the Seaman's Church Institute and St. Paul's, identifying them as rescue vehicles. The men volunteered ice and food and supplies of all kinds and their exhausted selves for ten days, until other services took over. Greg is proud of the role that he and Carmine's could play.

Looking ahead, what's the 100-year anniversary date? Will there be a celebration?

"You better believe it!," says Greg. "The date's under discussion and everyone's invited . . . maybe it'll last a week, maybe a month."

   – *Terry Walton, Seaport Magazine 2002, South Street Seaport Museum*
   Painting by Naima Rauam

★ *Changes with time – Carmine's at age 105 now has a spruced up exterior, and still draws its lively waterfront crowd.*

City of Austin *in two tides: with* Liberté *alongside at near dead low . . . and at high tide with starboard side of her deck just under water. . . . Still-graceful sterns of three Port Johnston sailing vessels are bleached white above the high-tide mark. Vessels are, from left, five-masted barkentine* Molfetta, *built in Pascagoula, Miss., in 1920; seagoing barge* James Howard, *built decades ago in South Freeport, Me., and once possibly schooner-rigged; and five-masted auxiliary barkentine* City of Austin, *built in 1918 at Orange, Tex. All carried cargoes into our harbors before being laid up here.*

The Muddy Foreshore –
South Street to Port Johnston
On a Wintry Harbor Day

Explorations of our harbor shore still holding old square-riggers and weathered brown barges, but losing them to time.

Winds 30-40 knots with gusts to 50. Seas four to six feet. All diminishing Monday with the possibility of snow flurries Tuesday. . . ."

It was a mid-January Sunday afternoon and the Coast Guard's 21.82 MHz voice recited imperturbably the specifications of what I could see: sunlit green seas close together sweeping northwest up the harbor, with long white crests. Tug bows socking into waves, throwing spray. People walking streets ashore only for essential reasons, holding hats, or maybe younger ones venturing out for the glory of wrestling with big weather in the city.

It was a splendid Sunday. We had planned a harbor voyage on Monday from South Street to Port Johnston, seven miles away down Staten Island's Kill Van Kull (Kill is from the Dutch word *kil*, for channel, I discovered. And Kull means haddock!).

Port Johnston is a muddy stretch of shore where old wooden sailing ships were long ago left to die. I had heard in particular of the five-masted barkentine *City of Austin*, still there to be seen. But how could such a ship be in our harbor in my time?

The 30-40 knots abated that night as foretold. Monday was good. We departed Pier 15, at mid-morning in deference to the tide, aboard the 35-foot ketch *Liberté*. South Street's ship historian Norman Brouwer had brought the most recent charts 369 and 285 and some knowledge of what our explorations were to be. Volunteer and trustee Dick Rath stocked the pot-bellied stove below against the 34 degrees up on deck. *Liberté's* owner Tom Ward progressed from shirt to sweater to jacket to immense parka as we left Pier 15 astern and neared the Battery. Soon we were out of the lee of Manhattan. I handed coffee all around.

The harbor was alive with tugs, ferries, lighters, and all sorts of other workboats. Governors Island lay well ahead to port, and New Jersey's hills and several of the harbor's other islands were all visible ahead and to starboard, brightened by sun. They were sharp in detail because of Sunday's clearing winds.

Chart 369 said *Liberté* could pass fairly close to the Statue of Liberty's island. Two flashing bells marked shoaling from 56 to 21 feet here, but this was caution only for the harbor's giant vessels. Our mark near Staten Island's northeast shore, where the strait Kill Van Kull runs between the island and New Jersey's city Bayonne, was Robbins Reef Lighthouse. Staten Island ferry passengers run by this lovely old light structure on every trip. Nearing it I wondered how soon it would be replaced by a highly efficient erector-set tower, the sort built with no pretense of grace. Never, I hoped.

Now, the upper bay lay astern and the lighthouse ahead. The wind had freshened to 20 knots or so, catching us just forward of abeam, pushing us steadily to port. It was *cold!*

The tug *Margaret M. McAllister* passed us by busily. We envied her assurance, because the navigational marks here differ somewhat from those on the chart. *Liberté* took a safer, slightly longer route leaving the lighthouse to starboard, and into the channel to Kill Van Kull.

In the channel everything changed. Three knots of tide pushed squarely against our bow. The engine worked hard. The wind added its resistance bow-on now, funneled efficiently between Bayonne and Staten Island's hilly shore. Each of us silently wondered what our situation might be if the wind kept freshening. We hadn't yet arrived, much less started home.

And then ahead I could see the Port Johnston hulks jutting up, sterns at odd angles, weary hulls sunk deep in mud but still with recognizable lines. The *City of Austin* lay nearest. Her masts were long missing. Her rail was rotten and gone in many places. She looked what she was – a ship from another time forever abandoned.

Liberté ventured close. Imperceptibly the mud received her keel and we were firmly caught. Quick backing freed us. We went alongside to tie up.

Salvage barge The Diver, *built by Capt. William A. Van Frank, is berthed here at Port Johnston, shoreward of near-gone hulks. . . .* City of Austin's *bow, still full of grace and detail, safely above high water.*

Aboard *City of Austin* we moved most cautiously. She lay well over to starboard, and the near part of her deck, under water at high tide but not submerged now, wore a slippery green coat that was treacherous underfoot. Huge sections of the deck were rotted away now, revealing muddy low-tide water in the hold below. Water poured out of her hull as the tide dropped.

There was beauty left here. Sunlight warmed the old wood's grains, in scuppers and portholes, in hefty deck beams and tiny plugs filling the holes above her deck fastenings. Chainplates, fully covered by brown underwater growing things, still stood aligned where once they had secured her rigging. Along *City of Austin's* other side lay the *James Howard,* the line of her upright bow still intact, the straight sides of her cargo hatches converging

Cargo hatches of James Howard; *looking aft toward Kill Van Kull.* City of Austin *lies at left,* Molfetta *at right.*

200 feet distant at her stern. And everywhere were ghosts of sea things – parts of a mast collar, a ring where once men secured a hatch-cover strongback, a round hole whose deck-light once let light below. Our discoveries seemed intimate ones.

Later, weary after climbing, I stretched out below on *Liberté*, eyes closed, thinking on artist John Noble's 1937 description of Port Johnston's beginnings, years before that:

"Port Johnston was once a terminal of the Central Railroad of New Jersey at whose docks for many years vessels loaded coal. Sometime after the World War it was abandoned and around the old piers were gathered, jibboom overhanging quarter, an odd assortment of craft from far and near. Long

Fittings jut out of City of Austin's *hefty deck beams (top), bared as her deck planking rots and drifts away with each tide. . . . Below on* City of Austin *(above), looking toward bow in flooded hold. Sunlight comes below through main cargo hatch, revealing deck stanchions and steel reinforcing beams.*

Old wood's grains lie highlighted by sun through rail chock opening (left), fitting long gone, and through scuppers (center). Drift pin juts up from City of Austin's *rotted starboard rail (right). Vessel is positively identified through her registration number 217160, seen here still clearly carved in thwartships beam of cargo hatch.*

Noank barges and great, ugly Gulf Coast barkentines were tied side to side with the examples of the finest shipbuilding turned out on the Maine coast. Some of the vessels were laid up all too soon; some were so old that the wonder is they reached the graveyard at all. . . ."

And now even the graveyard is nearly gone. Metal fittings have long been stripped off and sold. Masts are all scrapped or fallen. Every tide works on every hulk, taking away a plank, or hiding one more infinitesimal part in the mud of the shore.

Belowdecks on *Liberté*, eyes closed. My return to reality came with the ship's cat, who jumped from the tall companionway ladder down on my unsuspecting middle. The explorers were returning. Time to get underway.

We wanted to see Shooter's Island, a small chunk of land at the confluence of Newark Bay and the western end of Kill Van Kull, itself a wholly different graveyard of hulks. Tide and wind had eased. The channel was clearly marked. The island's muddy shores were invisible behind rows not of grand old sailing ships but of barges and tugs, all also left to rot, all also weathered a rich old brown.

We rounded Shooter's Island quickly, exclaiming over the extraordinarily deep underbody of a small beached tug, or figuring how soon the sun would take away our remaining warmth.

I felt oddly chastened for not knowing before now how fine a documentation of history lay lining this offshoot of my harbor.

Heading home we passed again beneath the arching Bayonne Bridge and again past the strange sights along the Kill Van Kull shores. The ferris wheel and other amusements of Bayonne's Playland, Norman showed us, all sit atop a string of old barges sunk so low now that they are part of the shore. Their deck structures are weathered to the water side, and bright pink toward the land. Further on, old ferry slips jutted out on both sides of the Kill. Then again came *City of Austin* and her ancient company, and opposite, to starboard, the handsome buildings of Sailor's Snug Harbor.

Nearing the mouth of the Kill we passed through Constable Hook Reach. Modern tankers today discharge oil there, where once square-riggers loaded case oil for the lamps of China.

And opposite the Reach we saw a once-elegant survivor of Staten Island's Colonnade Row, the 19th century columned mansions in which, Norman knew, Southern planters escaped the South's summer heat.

Ahead now, marking our return to the harbor's less secret parts, lay the Staten Island ferry slips and Robbins Reef Lighthouse. We angled out of the channel and across the darkening harbor toward South Street.

Liberté reached Pier 15 in full darkness and well below freezing weather. We secured her for the night and then went below, for talk and medicinal rum all around.

– Terry Walton, South Street Reporter 1975, South Street Seaport Museum

Port Johnston hulls once lay up Kill Van Kull and around behind Staten Island.

Kill Van Kull traffic rumbles steadily by (above), while egrets raise their families (left) and leave their signs. . . . Phlox proliferate amid ship timbers (below), late summer. Earlier that year, in May (below right), egret chicks wobbled their heads at an observer while their mothers protested loudly overhead.

Three species of egret were found on Shooter's Island at last count, in June of 1977, by the New Jersey Audubon Society: Snowy Egret (as here), Cattle Egret, and a single Great Egret. Counters saw ample populations also of Glossy Ibis and Black-Crowned Night Heron.

Shooter's Island –
Progress Passed It By, but Egrets Didn't

TODAY – Shooter's Island (1979) remains a thriving egret rookery behind Staten Island, along Kill Van Kull.

Shooter's Island is an uninhabited thirty-five-acre patch of land lying in the Kills behind Staten Island, just west of the mouth of Newark Bay. It has made news lately because of Staten Island Congressman John Murphy's proposal to remove it to widen the ship channel in the Kill Van Kull, and counter efforts by wildlife conservationists to preserve the Island as one of our area's very few nesting sites for snowy and cattle egrets, black-crowned night herons, and other long-legged wading birds.

The Island's name comes from colonial times, when, historians say, it was a popular place for hunting expeditions. During the Revolution it was used as a rendezvous and information drop by the spy network operating around British-occupied New York. The Island was then less than half its present size. . . .

Of the island's active Civil War and World War I shipyard buildings very little remains. Nature has reclaimed the Island with impressive thoroughness. Much of it is nearly impenetrable, except of course to the Norway rats and the nesting birds that inhabit it now. Grasses, bushes, and vines envelop concrete platforms that once supported power plants and machine shops. Thirty-foot ailanthus trees and birches jut out of thick carpets of vines, which in turn conceal the remains of shipyard buildings. Weeds and wildflowers grow everywhere – from piles of ash and clinkers, from rotten timbers of old scows, from cracks in concrete foundations. Off the west shore the vegetation on several barges lying clustered together has assumed the appearance of an extension of the Island, with thick grasses, bushes, and even thriving small trees with their roots reaching deep into the old timbers. Shooter's Island is – today, with its birds, hulks, and triumphant weeds – a mixture of harbor histories.

– From an article by Norman Brouwer, Seaport 1979, South Street Seaport Museum

---

★ *Changes with time – Shoreline wrecks from the island's turn-of-the-century and World War II shipbuilding eras have disappeared under opportunistic shrubbery, extending the island's acreage. Among famous vessels built here – the Kaiser's yacht* Meteor III *and the transatlantic racer* Atlantic. *Today the egrets remain safe in their protected rookery.*

Fulton Street looking west, c 1882 . . .
Plain East River shore just south of the
Bridge (1974) . . . Fulton Ferry ships
docked at Pier 1, near Fulton Landing;
towers and cranes across the river . . .
Ships along Furman Street, Pier 2.

Fulton Ferry Brooklyn . . .
Our River's Other Shore

TODAY – Fulton Ferry Brooklyn (1974), just south of the bridge, is a centerpiece of waterfront renaissance. See Changes with time, below.

Explore this accidental but wonderful survival in our age of concrete-and-steel sidewalk curbs and undecorated buildings . . .

It was a sunny mid-morning in the fall, as I neared Fulton Ferry Brooklyn again, from my house just up the hill. I thought of Innkeeper Cornelius Dircksen's tiny vessel, the 1642 ferry to "Breuckelen," pulled ashore there ages ago. And of the cattle herded down to cross in the scows. And of the ferry drownings, the outrage at the Fulton-Cutting ferry monopoly two centuries later, the old life at the Bankers' Corner at 25-27 Fulton, the clatter of goods-carts come to 19th century market. It was all here over time, at the same river and the same shore. But of course it's all vastly altered now, and what the city must deal with in its redoings is Fulton Street today. . . .

At the foot of Fulton stood the Fulton Ferry Fire Boat House, upright and diminutive replacement of its ornate Victorian forebear. Just north in the old hotel building was the Waterfront Restaurant, where truckers and longshoremen have early breakfasts. The river was right there, and at its edge a Pier 1 vessel's bow jutted up, so I could not see South Street on the opposite shore. . . .

"The river was right there, and at its edge a Pier 1 vessel's bow jutted up, so I could not see South Street on the opposite shore. . . ."

Just north of the Fire Boat pier the *chuff-chunk* sounds and steamings of a pile driver meant that new bulkheading had begun. The Bridge loomed over its street. . . . I stood awhile to watch trucks thunder by – "Perdue Chickens," "Porky Suckling Pigs," "Yellow Freight System Inc." – all headed for Furman Street and the docks. Along Fulton there I saw city busses waiting at their turnarounds, before heading back across Brooklyn. . . . At Elizabeth Street, I noticed the giant granite blocks forming a crosswalk, curb to curb, with Belgian blocks carefully patterned along them.

Inside the Waterfront Restaurant over coffee, its owner, Phil Rando, spoke of the Fulton Ferry prints that Banker's Trust's walls show in their Montague Street branch. He told me of his own pictures – newspaper clippings of what it was like here years ago, and promised to bring them in. He took me outside ("I'll bet you haven't seen *this!*") and there, where a second-floor window pediment is missing, are the capital letters NU or NO, hidden since the time the pediments were added, during renovations in the 1860s. Whatever did they once name? He told me of the extra hours and the fixing up he'll do when people begin to come to Fulton Street again. . . .

– *Terry Walton, from South Street Reporter 1974, South Street Seaport Museum*

★ *Changes with time – Today, Fulton Ferry Brooklyn is the centerpiece of Brooklyn Bridge Park, a new 1.3 mile, 85 acre park being created along the shoreline between the Manhattan Bridge and Pier 6. Brooklyn resident and waterfront advocate Cindy Goulder doesn't expect Fulton Landing itself to change much, but the waterfront to its north and south will be transformed into landscaped lawns, sports courts, paths, and plazas.*

Fleur de lis window grill . . . granite and Belgian block crosswalk . . . Bridge and Fulton Ferry Bank . . . Brooklyn Eagle . . . the Bank . . . doorway . . . griffin beneath the Eagle Warehouse arch.

Journal of East River Traffic, 1883

There is between the city of New York and the city of Brooklyn an arm of the sea called the East River. . . . Day and night, summer and winter, an endless procession of ships, steamboats, canal-boats, schooners, sloops, and barges sails or steams along this arm of the sea. It is like a Broadway upon the water, crowded with traffic. There comes a fussy little tug, toiling along with four great schooners deep laden with coal. They have come from the coal depots at Jersey City, and are bound East. There is a big, lazy sloop, with a cargo of red bricks. The tide runs swift and strong, and the waves leap in white clouds of spray from the sharp bows of flying steamboats, or roll in surging billows from the black stems of huge merchantmen. It is like a bit of the great sea, with a city on either side. ★ There are more people living by the banks of this arm of the sea than in any other place on this continent. Nearly half a million people cross this rough, swift-flowing water every day; and though the ferry-boats are among the largest and best in the world, the little voyage is at times long and dangerous. Fogs sometimes delay the boats for hours, and floating ice in winter often blocks the way so that navigation is almost suspended. – *Charles Bernard, 1883 from The Brooklyn Bridge*

Look at the Buildings
Of Waterfront New York

TODAY – The harbor's waterfront buildings (1977) are treasured as handsome connections between two centuries. See Changes with time, below.

Get out on the water here! An old brick warehouse, an elaborately gatewayed steel ferry terminal, a ship's-bell-chiming, clock-towered fireboat pier tiny against the city's heights. . . . Here is an appreciative look, a discovery with untrained eyes.

There is, for the building-watcher in New York, a treasure in structures waiting, salted away along the shoreline of the harbor. The waterfront buildings that I mean are from another time, mostly, when ferries and railroads ran everywhere. When coastal schooners were a common sight, when steam freighters had long proven their worth to our port.

⭐

"When they were built, these buildings from an earlier time, they were common in being meant to please the spirit of people who looked at them, whether to work there or to pass by."

⭐

When they were built, these buildings from an earlier time, they were common in being meant to please the spirit of people who looked at them, whether to work there or to pass by. They have arched windows and decorated lintels, and are made of brick, stone, wood, and steel. Differing textures enliven their surfaces. Contrasting-colored quoins march up their edges.

They have served to warehouse Hudson River coal and West Indies sugar. Or welcomed ferry passengers to the city through their monumental arches. Or received tug-drawn floats of railroad cars, full of molasses fresh from the Brooklyn sugar refineries and destined for inland markets.

They have thus had, generally, one or a series of single uses, comprehensible as "ferry terminal" or "sugar warehouse" or "recreation pier." And they have a rather comforting human scale.

It was to find and photograph some of these waterfront buildings that we set out in the Museum's small inboard skiff, used on other days to teach boat handling to our Pioneer Marine School students. It was a bright hot summer Saturday.

Four elated staffmembers strong, we had noted the Fulton Fish Market men hosing off the sidewalks along Fulton Street. At the piers we had seen the schooner *Pioneer's* passengers board for a harbor sail. Celebratory flags flew from one of *Peking's* masts. Families of sparrows carefully inspected the pier timbers.

Almost unfairly, our earliest destination was the Empire Stores complex in Brooklyn, just across the East River from South Street and just north of the Brooklyn Bridge. Unfairly, because here is a lovely row of arch-windowed brick warehouses that seem at last to be off the endangered list, unlike so much else we would see that day.

Within the last year, moving symbiotically with restoration plans for the rest of the Fulton Ferry neighborhood, plans for a tasteful mix of commercial/cultural redevelopment for Empire Stores have ignited people's thoughts about them. Newspapers write of the warehouses. Books carry appreciative photographs of them. Volunteers think fondly of them. Dreamers present schemes for them.

South Ferry's grand steel arches (detail, right) welcome passengers from Staten Island and Governors Island, in the harbor's only surviving ferry runs. The terminal was completed in 1909 and ran its ferries to South Brooklyn for nearly 30 years.

The discovery has begun, and it fits well with general waterfront plans of long standing.

Though at first glance a single grand structure, Empire Stores is actually a series of seven warehouses sharing one continuous brick facade of arched windows and doors rather rhythmically placed. They parallel the river close by and offer a long sweep of shore that would be wonderful for benches someday.

The smaller early 19th century warehouses on the site were destroyed by fire more than a century ago, and the successors were built in 1870-1885 for storing raw materials – like sugar from the West Indies, or coffee beans from South America. The ships that docked here are of the common but vanished sort caught in historic photographs – coastal schooners from Maine, brigantines from the West Indies.

Think of a city dweller's joy already, in exploring the Fulton Ferry Brooklyn neighborhood. Its elements thus far – not even counting the grand sight of all lower Manhattan just across the river – include many-windowed loft apartments, a new park, an elegant restaurant built out

over the water, and a historical society conducting research and serving as a catalyst for the whole renascence of the neighborhood.

In warm weather, NMHS (National Maritime Historical Society, long an ally in South Street's work) has begun to draw families down for concerts and exhibits at the river's edge. A former fireboat house serves now as headquarters for the new life of the place.

Not so bright at all in its future, however, but full of curious old maritime structures, is Wallabout Bay. It was here, just upriver from the Empire Stores site, that American soldiers died by the thousands on British prison ships during the Revolution. Now as we poked around in the Museum skiff we could see shore grass and determined trees growing right out of the bulkheads. A ship was berthed for repairs. An odd wooden shed towered over us on long steel legs, the super-structure of an obsolete device that once bridged the levels of tide and shore for railroad-car floats. An aged wooden dry-dock, a 3,200 gallons-per-minute wonder in its day, lay ahead. To port we noticed a handsome stone tunnel, a final outflow in the city's storm sewer system, unappreciated for all its tapered granite good looks.

Lackawanna passenger ferries to Hoboken left this clock-towered terminal at West 23rd Street (top) built at the turn of the century and demolished decades later in favor of freight piers. Berenice Abbott's photograph was taken in 1935. . . . At the run's other end passengers disembarked at similarly embellished terminal, still standing today. . . . Elegant rails, arches and pediments intermix with patched cement on both water and land facades, but the structure is beautiful still.

On shore, an abandoned power station's severe brick facade had presented its round-arched windows and other pleasing detail for well over half a century. Coal barges had discharged cargo here for ready transformation to electricity for the city. A coal chute still jutted right across the windows, rudely it seemed. (In Baltimore, staffmember Norman Brouwer mentioned, a power station not so different from this one was now a center for shops and waterside loft apartments. What might the future hold for ours?)

As we left Wallabout Bay, helmsman and Pioneer Marine School Director Roger Kreutzer noticed an all too camouflaged sight in the bulkhead, not far from the tunnel. It was a young and frightened German shepherd, lying wedged in a crevice just below the high tide mark. He responded to our offers of help with very believable warning growls. We left him, called the harbor police, who said they'd be right along, and proceeded.

Now came a glorious run downriver under the Brooklyn Bridge. Past Empire Stores and the little Brooklyn fireboat house to port. Past South Street and Wall Street to starboard, and to South Ferry, on southernmost Manhattan.

Here the three grand arches of the ferry terminal welcome passengers into New York from Governors Island. The building was completed in 1909, with its structure and ornament inherited, we learned, from the Eiffel Tower in Paris. But the Tower is of course an open steel framework, and here the facade of the South Ferry terminal's steel framework is filled in and painted a copper green, with the very rivets forming part of the pattern of geometric lights and darks. It is truly an awesome structure from water level, as it was meant to be, and it is equaled by its own landside facade with a wholly different pattern.

Structurally different but similarly awesome were the copper-sheathed ferry terminals once standing at West 23rd Street and Liberty Street, Hudson River. One grand counterpart to these still stands: the Erie Lackawanna rail and passenger terminal in Hoboken.

Earlier small-scale buildings near the South Ferry site, long gone now but still surviving into skyscraper decades, came to light as we pored through old photographs later. Among them, the granite Romanesque Barge Office, Engine Company No. 57's ornate wooden fireboat station that once stood behind Pier A, and the filigree-railed final station of the El.

Not so far from South Ferry's terminal but around on Manhattan's Hudson River tip, we took the boat in close to see Pier A itself, another once-threatened waterfront structure. Late morning light showed us the detail of its clock-tower. The vertical lines in its facade were set off pleasingly against similar but soaring lines in the World Trade Center towers.

Two years ago it was declared that Battery Park City landfill needs would require Pier A's demolition. But now the diminutive ninety-three-year-old artifact will keep its place at the island's tip – as a city landmark. Research and restoration money are in hand to this end. Alongside Pier A we saw fireboats *John H. Glenn Jr, Harry M. Archer,* and *John D. McKean* docked, at the ready.

Fully around on the Hudson side now, we looked at the older pier structures along both of the river's shores. Pier 58's federal pediments still preside over its now paneless windows. (International Mercantile Marine Co. once discharged passengers and general freight here.) Decrepit but still handsome too is Pier C, its classic detail still visible, still pleasing.

Pier 43 replaced a recreation pier in the 1930s. Pier 42 still carried its covered shed when the 205-foot square-rigged ship *Christian Radich* docked there for the first Operation Sail, in 1964. Today the New York City vocational schoolship *John W. Brown* berths there and city people work on summer tans alongside, where the shed once was. Upriver, we noted, other water seekers fish off Pier 74.

Soon came sandwiches and Cokes underway, with conversation and mouthfuls always interrupted by the sight of one more discovery ashore. We headed over now to examine Hoboken's seventy-year-old Erie Lackawanna ferry terminal. It resembles South Ferry and has six waterside arches with an ornamental rail all along their top, floral and geometric patterns on both land and water sides, and columns, towers, and pediments as well. One of the arches is falling into the river. The lovely rail is partly gone. And patched plain cement walls intrude. But our excitement at examining an elegant artifact like this, unknown to most of us till now, was undiminished.

> ★
>
> *"Wouldn't it be good indeed*
> *for New York's spirit to wonder*
> *who put handsome rails*
> *on lighthouses?"*
>
> ★

Heading downriver now we slowed to admire the ten-story-tall building beside the Colgate factory, established in 1874 in Jersey City, New Jersey. It is a white-painted reinforced concrete structure whose single row of arched windows tops several rows of squared ones below, and creates a lovely sense of columns on the facade. (Beside it, atop the smaller and also attractive Colgate factory itself, sits the world's largest clock of the conventional kind – fifty-three years old, fifty feet in diameter, with its minute-hand nearly twenty-six feet long.)

Next in our explorations we came upon the slate-roofed and dormered Central Railroad of New Jersey terminal. It is eighty-eight years old now and nearly hidden behind aged freight sheds and car float bridges, so our looking was tantalizingly restricted. But soon the CRNJ terminal will be restored as part of New Jersey's Liberty State Park plans, we learned, and the obtrusive sheds will be gone.

Nearly obscured here by time, and its upriver twin destroyed by fire soon after this summer 1977 photograph was taken: sheet-metal-clad Lackawanna Railroad Pier 4 (Jersey City) manages nevertheless the grace of columns and classic symmetry.

Unequivocally now, we were running out of time. Roger took us up adeptly along the New Jersey shore, past Ellis Island's ornately quoined and towered buildings, past the crumbling railroad piers at Greenville and Communipaw, past Liberty State Park itself, alongshore just behind the Statue of Liberty. Out we went now to Robbins Reef lighthouse.

The lighthouse itself is the only one left in our inner harbor. Another one stands on Lighthouse Hill in Staten Island, and an unused one (the subject of the delightful children's book *The Little Red Lighthouse and the Great Gray Bridge*) still stands along the Hudson beneath the George Washington Bridge.

I noticed the graceful detail of stanchions of the rail surrounding the Robbins Reef light-house top. Why put ornament way out in mid-harbor, where no one can see it? Wonderful force of habit? Or to please the lighthouse keeper?

I was struck with the shortness of time both in this day and in the prospects of structures like this lighthouse, or the elegant Erie Lackawanna terminal, or the Empire Stores warehouses if the new plans somehow do not happen. Wouldn't it be good indeed for New York's spirit to wonder who put handsome rails on lighthouses? To wonder who designed pier buildings not with efficient undecorated lines but with pleasing detail and human scale? Who used these structures two generations or another century ago, and for what? What ships? What captains? What commerce?

A last stop on our explorations, we now had to decide, would be Erie and Atlantic basins, over again in Brooklyn and not far down the harbor from South Street. Staten Island, with its ferry terminal at St. Georges and its inactive but gear-strewn Coast Guard lighthouse depot at Tompkinsville, would receive complete neglect until another day.

Brooklyn's Erie Basin warehouses are among the loveliest I have ever seen. They are still

The Old Hotel
At 92 South Street

With Sloppy Louie's on its ground floor – and sawdust on the floor of Sloppy Louie's – the Old Hotel at 92 South Street earned a chapter in Joe Mitchell's beloved book *The Bottom of the Harbor*. I knew Joe Mitchell enough to walk around South Street with him occasionally, ate in Sloppy Louie's lots of times with lots of smiles from Louie, and found these charcoal drawings of the Old Hotel's rooms absolutely beautiful. They are by local artist Naima Rauam, generous and skilled and beloved to all who know her.

In his book, Joe Mitchell talks to Louie Marino about the hotel's boarded up rooms, and Louie says he doesn't know what's in them: "I've heard this and I've heard that, but I don't know. I wish to God I did know. I've wondered often enough. I've rented this building twenty-two years, and I've never been above the second floor. The reason being, that's as far as the stairs go." But Naima got up there! Sloppy Louie's is long departed, but *The Bottom of the Harbor* is readily available from Amazon.com; it is a treasure.

– *Terry Walton*

Old Rooms

"Many of the buildings at the South Street Seaport date back to the early 1800s. Some housed wholesale seafood dealers of the Fulton Fish Market until 2005. While the facades of these buildings often kept up with changing times, upstairs time has stood still in some old rooms which have been neglected. ★ *"The haunting emptiness of the rooms inspired me to do these charcoal drawings. Morning light, softened by window panes not cleaned for decades, falls on ancient floors and plaster walls crumbling with age. The brightness seems to coax the years from the shadows, and offers me a connection to the history, and the stories, within these fragile spaces."* – Naima Rauam

5 Favorite Harbor Places –
From Handsome Brick & Grand Old Stone
To Harbor School, Harbor Sails, & a Hudson Destination

Schermerhorn Row, Centerpiece in Brick

Time was, merchant and ship owner Peter Schermerhorn built this handsome 1812 "counting house" row to warehouse goods eagerly received from sailing ships – the square-riggers just at the foot of Fulton Street. Cascades of uses and then decades of neglect followed, and time forgot the place. ★ One evening in 1966, when I first ventured down to help take next steps for South Street Seaport Museum, founded the following year, I didn't quite know where I was going (prior meetings were mostly uptown). Fulton Street was dark and dingy down near the East River. The air was properly redolent of Fish Market fish. Belgian blocks rattled my taxi stem to stern. The driver turned and said to me, "Lady, are you sure you want to be down here? It's really a rough place." ★ Well, I found the dreamers meeting, South Street got founded, and I got familiar with Sloppy Louie's, Sweet's, the Schermerhorn Row's creaky floorboards, the Fish Market across the street, and the ships newly returned to the foot of the street. Today Schermerhorn Row is all cleaned up and sparkling, a Museum centerpiece, with intriguing maritime exhibits and the surrounds of nightlife lively late in neighboring eateries. But I remember that first dark, taxi-rattling night. And I remember the breathtaking beauty of Schermerhorn Row, then and now. – *Terry Walton*

★

Just off the Battery . . . A Second September Sail

It has been five years since I happened upon an experience that will always stay with me – a beautiful September sail on New York's lower Hudson River, in the middle of the night. The wind was at least 15 knots, the air warm at summer's end, yet with a hint of autumn ahead. The water, alive and lapping. And it was September 11, 2002 – an

TERRY WALTON

144

anniversary that my friends and I wanted to acknowledge with reverence. A sail seemed the right tribute. ★ The intended outing took place in early evening just off the Battery. We sailed little J24 sloops out of the Manhattan Yacht Club's North Cove Marina. We were tiny white sails moving slowly against the enormous backdrop of Lower Manhattan. It was beautiful, a tranquil observance. A completion to the day. ★ Afterwards, eight of us sat outside near North Cove for an impromptu dinner. Invigorated by the sail, and now joined by lively gusts that it seems one finds only on the west side of Manhattan, we had a festive meal filled with energy and laughter and the excitement of being utterly absorbed in a perfect evening. We were all exactly where we wanted to be on that occasion, in that moment. Even long after dinner was finished, we lingered, wanting the night to continue. And when the gusts suddenly picked up, one in the group declared that we should join him for a late-night sail on his new fifty-foot sloop. We didn't hesitate. ★ The big sloop maneuvered gracefully out of North Cove and into the feisty river. While the sky was dark, lower Manhattan was lit with the powerful luminous beams commemorating the missing Towers. That night, the beams filled a void in our city and in our lives. They illuminated our way for a time as we headed north up the Hudson. ★ I wasn't used to the size of this new boat, but its strength seemed absolutely appropriate to match the conditions of the water, and of this powerful

night. Our course took us past tremendous cargo barges, asleep mid-river for the evening. The huge, lit-up Colgate Clock, NJ Central's grandly restored railroad terminal, the black-netted golf range of Chelsea Piers, the barnacled *Frying Pan* lightship, the tremendous deck of the *Intrepid* – all of these familiar landmarks fell behind us as we tacked north. The wind was brisk and steady and the lights ashore lined our back-and-forth course. This was an adventure we had not planned, and all the more beautiful for that. ★ Eventually, we reached the George Washington Bridge, whose light show we sailed beneath in awe. Beside us now to starboard was the little lighthouse that I remembered my mom reading to me about as a child. And throughout the night, tacking upriver and then running down, we shared the emotional reminder of our once-familiar skyline glaringly, shockingly altered forever. ★ This second September sail took us into 2 a.m. the next morning. I went to work later that day and tried to tell the story. I wanted to convey all that was special about our time, yet it was beyond mere words. It was a magical experience in which eight people embraced a beautiful night, in honor. – *Jenifer Walton*

NOTE – This evening sail was followed just three days later by the New York Harbor Sailing Foundation's "Sail for America" gathering, in which more than 1,200 boats sailed in the harbor to honor those lost on 9/11.

★

The NY Harbor School –
New Perspectives in Learning

Imagine a school where the passion for learning is as alive as the harbor. Such is the theme for the New York Harbor School (NYHS), which opened with a hundred twenty-five students in September 2003, far from the waterfront in Bushwick, Brooklyn, and soon will move to Governors Island. ★ This innovative public high school prepares its students, now tripled to three hundred seventy-five,

with the traditional high school curriculum – but also presents a wide-ranging exploration of the harbor through a rigorous four-year maritime course. By graduation, students are

proficient in the traditional English-History-Math-Science studies, per New York State requirements, but they've also had life-changing experiences out on the water and along its shores. ★ The Harbor School's introductory course acquaints incoming freshmen with their harbor. Sophomore year brings Maritime Technology (navigation, marine communication, boat building, et al) and Harbor Arts (literary and visual arts inspired by the local

"I didn't know what organisms lived in the harbor. Then I found out about things that consume and produce, and the bacteria in the water. This class has taught me a lot about the harbor and the estuary. It has shown me how much people pollute in the harbor, and that changed me because now I don't litter or dump any waste in the harbor. This semester I have learned about algae and oxygen. . . ."

waterfronts). Junior and Senior years bring final high school studies, and then internships within the marine industry. Students experience harbor life through hands-on work in diverse areas such as

*"I was the first one to volunteer to eat oysters.
I felt so strange, then I just gulped it down like nothing."*

*"My understanding has gotten way better since I
started taking this class. . . . In this semester I've
learned that the marine animals benefit the ocean more
than us people benefit the land."*

From NY Harbor School Students –

Take one, one off! Take four, four off! Take two, two off!" The captain gave out the commands to remove the dock lines. By now we only had a stern spring line on the starboard side. The captain made stern way off the stern spring, the bow came over to port. "Take three!" he yelled and off we were on our new adventures. . . .

Down the North River and up the East River we went, bound for Long Island Sound. With the *Lettie G.* running on motor power, night arrived and darkness drew upon us. Our navigation lights and running lights on, I stood watch at the helm. A feeling drew upon me as my watch and I were in full control of the majestic 125-foot vessel. . . .

I remembered the first time I was at the helm. I was nervous with the captain studying my every move, instructing me where to go, how to handle the boat. I was scared. I had never felt this sort of responsibility. Now look at me, in charge of the vessel all by myself. Appointed Senior Watch Officer, so much responsibility in my hands, so much power. The wind shifted to port. I turned to compensate and reach a better angle and to allow the *Lettie G. Howard* to gain greater speed. . . .

– From an article by Jeffrey Rodriguez, aboard schooner Lettie G. Howard,
in a cooperative program with South Street Seaport Museum

the lightship at various locations, a few months here, a few months there, even a few months anchored upriver near Grant's Tomb – until he hit on a brilliant idea: A 330-foot former railroad barge was available (very used, of course). He immediately bought it to use as a floating dock for his lightship. It is reported that when he came home that evening, he said to his wife Angela, "Honey, I just bought a barge" – and she just smiled. ★ After putting "a little work" into the barge in Staten Island – including an entire new deck – he had a tugboat bring the barge to his low rent waterside paradise at the foot of West 23rd Street and the Hudson River, and shortly after tied his lightship up alongside. Thus began the legend of "Pier 63 Maritime," as he then named the barge. ★ Pier 63 Maritime grew in fits and starts. In time *Frying Pan* was joined by another historic vessel, the retired fireboat *John J. Harvey*, of which John was, of course, a part owner. Kayaks joined the mix, along with an assortment of other boats including the historic tugboats *Bertha* and *New York Central No. 13*. ★ Eventually beer-and-snacks sales grew into a full-service restaurant, café, and bar with great sunset and water views. Krevey was generous in making the barge available to non-profit organizations for public events, and the facility evolved into a popular Hudson River venue, with its eclectic mix of historic ships and visiting tall ships, harbor tours, music and movie evenings, kayak launches, outrigger canoe events, sunset gatherings, and

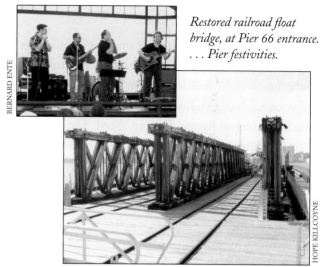

Restored railroad float bridge, at Pier 66 entrance. . . . Pier festivities.

diverse other public-welcoming activities. ★ In 2006 the venue was closed to make way for the construction of Hudson River Park, but not for too long. A new home for Pier 63 Maritime emerged three blocks north – the site of a restored historic "float bridge" pier once used to roll railroad cars ashore from barges just like John's. In fact it's likely that John's very barge, formerly a Lackawanna RR Company barge, landed at this same float bridge in a former life. ★ John Krevey's reborn Hudson River venture is now called Pier 66 Maritime and reopened on July 4th, 2008, at the foot of 26th Street, with the same dawn-to-dusk array of uses and the same ambience, and with the Lightship *Frying Pan* still berthed alongside. – *Capt. John Doswell, Working Harbor Committee*

★ ★ ★

"Working Harbor Day" – Exploring New York's Working Waterfront

Working Harbor Day – it's a maritime tradition now. On one recent Working Harbor Day, more than 3,000 New Yorkers and friends gathered at water's edge in mid-May – then went out on boats for low-priced Hidden Harbor Tours® to the harbor's little-known places. The instigator in this event? The Working Harbor Committee, six years old in 2008. Among the

destinations? The Kill Van Kull and Staten Island's active tug yards . . . the Hudson's bustling liner piers and restored and active New Jersey waterfront . . . the Brooklyn Navy Yard, Atlantic and Erie basins, and Jersey ship ports with their juxtaposition of derelict old vessels and thriving ship repair and container ship facilities. Participants saw it all from the water, and they loved it! Their first question once back ashore? . . . "When can we do this again?" ★ Well, mid-May is always the

★

"Experiencing the calmness of the water, the warmth of the weather which extended to the atmosphere within the boat. It was fabulously beautiful. . . . I have never experienced such peace of mind in New York City."
– Hidden Harbor Tours for seniors, Working Harbor Committee, 2006

★

time. On this annual day of harbor exploration, New Yorkers and New-Yorkers-for-a-Day discover fascinating facts about the harbor from which the city grew – a

harbor that is today full of surging life and energy. They visit behind-the-scenes piers, hear first-hand recollections from pilots, tug captains, historians, and more. They learn of the harbor's real challenges in assuring public access, as redevelopment progresses in parks, residential, and commercial spaces. They learn of plans for the working life force that sustains New York's trade with the world – such as the pressing need to accommodate the growth in cruise liner visits to our port, as well as facilities for container vessels bringing the goods that connect us with the nation. ★ Why is this knowledge important? Because, notes Capt. John Doswell of the Working Harbor Committee, New York is the East Coast's number one terminal for shipping of all kinds, from cocoa beans to cars to all manner of water-borne goods. ★ Some of the harbor's most intriguing places are explorable by land and others by boat, and others, vanished now, are found only in memory.

– Terry Walton, for the Working Harbor Committee

Hidden Harbor Story-Tellings

You'll find harbor historians who love their knowledge and seek to offer it to you, as an accompaniment to the *HarborGuide* itself. Their combined experiences and story-tellings could keep our tours running well beyond the day. They carry harbor history around in their absorbent minds, the yield of years of delving into creeks and streams, exploring backwaters and shoreline places, finding kinship with other harbor people, and of course their own harbor work.

> *– HarborGuide '04, Working Harbor Committee,*
> *Welcoming Hidden Harbor Tour participants*

The first America's Cup winner – in 1851 – was a schooner modeled after a New York harbor pilot boat of the time; she was captained in that first race by a member of the Sandy Hook Pilots.

★

The Staten Island ferry makes 104 trips a day and carries 65,000 passengers.

★

The tides in the North (Hudson) River reach as far north as Troy.

★

Red Hook in Brooklyn is the largest cocoa port in the U.S.

★

The last two major U.S. Navy ships built at the Brooklyn Navy Yard, both large aircraft carriers, had hinged mainmasts to enable them to pass under the Brooklyn Bridge for their sea trials.

★

The only borough of New York City that is not an island or part of an island is The Bronx.

★

The retired fireboat *John J. Harvey* can pump enough water to fill a home-sized swimming pool in 30 seconds.

★

After the September 11 terrorist attack on the World Trade Center more than 500,000 citizens were evacuated by volunteer working watercraft of New York harbor.

– Capt. John Doswell, Working Harbor Committee, 2008

★ ★ ★

Harbor Discoveries –
You Are Invited!

Harbor Voices is both celebration and invitation. For all my years as South Street Seaport Museum staff and later as Working Harbor Committee volunteer, it's been one unending and joyous harbor exploration for me. Most recently, it was harbor photographer Bernard Ente's Railmarine Tour that gave me close-up sightings of Hudson and East River rail connections all along the shores. They're still there, the restored Erie Lackawanna and handsome Jersey Central terminals, the rail car floats and roundabouts, the unmistakable evidences of the harbor as highway once connecting shore to shore in vital commerce. On that railmarine sleuthing day T-shirts and hats (Anthracite Rail Road Historical Society, Lackawanna 2038 Rail Road Express Agency, Chesapeake & Ohio Steam Locomotive/America's Last and Best, and Lehigh Valley Rail Road among their insignias) confirmed the deep and devoted knowledge of my fellow passengers. ★ This summer '08 excursion, one of many arranged by the Working Harbor Committee in partnership with other harbor organizations, was for me full of new understandings in all the old familiar places. The lists that follow – of harbor highlights to watch for and harbor-minded places to visit – invite your exploration. *TW*

New York Waterway
Home Port

Manhattan Cruise Terminal

Pier 86/Intrepid
• Circle Line Pier
• West 39th Street
Ferry Terminal

WEEHAWKEN

MANHATTAN

QUEENS

HOBOKEN

Pier 66 Maritime
Chelsea Piers

Erie Lackwana RR
Terminal

NEW JERSEY

Marine Company 1
FDNY

Hudson River

East River

Newtown Creek

• Pier 40

JERSEY CITY

Pier
25/26

Pier 16 & 17
South Street
/Fulton

Exchange Place

Morris Canal Turning Basin
Colgate Clock

Liberty State Park

Jersey Central RR Terminal

Marine Division
Headquarters, FDNY
(Brooklyn Navy Yard)

Caven Point
US Army Corps
of Engineers

Ellis
Island

Atlantic
Basin

Fulton Ferry
Brooklyn
/Brooklyn
Bridge

Liberty
Island

Governors
Island

Newark Bay

Cruise Terminal

Erie Basin

Beard Street Pier, Red Hook

BROOKLYN

Gowanus Canal

BAYONNE

Upper
New York Bay

Bayonne
Bridge to Port
Elizabeth

Kill Van Kull

Caddell
Dry Dock

St. George
Ferry Terminal

Moran
tugs

Reinauer
tugs

McAllister
tugs

Noble
Maritime/Snug
Harbor Center

STATEN ISLAND

Sandy Hook
Pilots Station

Verrazano-
Narrows
Bridge

Ft. Wadsworth
US Coast Guard
Vessel Traffic Service

World
Financial
Center

North
Cove

Battery
Park
City

South
Cove

South
Street
Seaport
Museum

Pier A

Pier 17

Pier 11

Battery
Park

Staten Island
Ferry
Terminal

LI Sound Down to NY Harbor . . .
An Age-Old Route

Traveling by small boat from Long Island's North Shore to New York City is always an adventure, one made even more compelling by the knowledge that you are following in the maritime footsteps of the captains of coastal traders, warships, and adventurers dating back to the age of explorers and then the colonial land-claimers and merchants who followed them.

I first made the East River voyage as a daytrip from Bayville in my 17-foot speedboat as a teenager when New York harbor was more threatening, with dirty water hiding floating pilings and other debris that could stave in a hull or rip off a stern-drive with much of the shoreline desolate, abandoned and littered with hulks and empty buildings.

Things got more commodious, albeit far slower, and the city more welcoming later on when I had traded up as an adult to a 31-foot sloop so we could stay overnight, usually in the lee of tall ships and Wall Street skyscrapers at South Street Seaport Museum.

My first run in with my O'Day 31, *Adele B.,* in 1986 was the most memorable of these trips, in part because we traveled down Long Island Sound in company with the replica H.M.S. *Bounty* and other tall ships en route to Op Sail. That really drove home the historic nature of our route.

The trip west is interesting also because of your proximity to other fragments of maritime history: the Sands Point, Execution Rocks, and Stepping Stones lighthouses. Then you pass the storied halls, and often the training ships, of the U.S. Merchant Marine Academy at the former Chrysler Estate in Kings Point to the south and the State University of New York Maritime College at the former Fort Schuyler to the north. The old fort property serves as the northern jumping off point for the Throgs Neck Bridge, and sailing under any large suspension bridge in a small craft is always eye-opening. The bridge marks the end of the Sound and beginning of the East River with historic stone Fort Totten to port.

Things get increasingly urban as you sweep under the Bronx-Whitestone Bridge before passing the runways of LaGuardia Airport and the sprawling barbed-wire-encased prison complex on Rikers Island. But I'm always even more fascinated by the next landmark, little known North Brother Island, where the haunting ruins of a city hospital still stand and where the burning excursion steamer *General Slocum* came to rest on June 15, 1904, in New York's worst maritime disaster with 1,021 deaths.

Next comes the once treacherous Hell Gate, with the chaos of currents tamed by the government's demolition of rocky outcroppings, but still a log flume ride in a small boat when the tide is running. After the confluence with the Harlem River to starboard comes the always impressive view of the high-rise Manhattan shoreline. To port is Roosevelt Island, with a lighthouse, condos, and ruins of another imposing city hospital.

Back on the Manhattan side, there's Gracie Mansion, the United Nations, Empire State Building, and the succession of soaring spans crowned by the Brooklyn Bridge and its framing of the amazing panorama of the Upper Bay and the Statue of Liberty.

All this less than a half day from home.

– *Bill Bleyer*

From left: East River sightings – Hell Gate Bridge . . . Newtown Creek observers . . . Manhattan Bridge . . . EPA vessel North River *headed to work . . . fireboat at Brooklyn Bridge, just north of South Street Seaport Museum.*

Shoreline Guide to the Hidden Harbor

At New York harbor's height in World War II, this was a very different place with more than a thousand piers. On one day in March 1943 there were 543 ships at anchor in the port, awaiting a berth or a convoy.... ★ As *Life* Magazine reminded readers in November 1944, "With its seven bays, four river mouths and four estuaries, it is by far the world's best and biggest natural harbor and most of the world's major ports could easily be tucked into it." Imagine the activity of all these ships! ... cargo unloaded onto piers, warehouses, barges, and railway cars ... tugs needed for moving barges and docking ships, lighters for

unloading ships at anchor ... dozens of ferry routes criss-crossing the harbor amidst frenetic activity. ★ The monarchs of this water were the great transatlantic liners – pride of their respective nations, made fast at their piers on North River in both Manhattan and Hoboken. No great city harbor in Europe could accommodate these magnificent liners – instead, passengers had to take a boat train from London, Paris, or Rome to the docks. ★ But in New York the docks were just a cab ride away. Our embracing harbor, as well, connected railroads from the west directly to Long Island and New England. And freight cars moved straight across the harbor by "car float" – special barges with rails. ★ Waterfront maps of the 1940s show most of New Jersey's shore from Staten Island to Edgewater (opposite 110th Street) taken up with active rail yards, as was the Brooklyn waterfront from the Navy Yard all the way to the Verrazano. Ours was truly a working waterfront with thousands of working watercraft each doing a job. ★ New York harbor is vastly quieter today. Only Cunard's *QM2* crosses the Atlantic [joined today by *Queen Victoria*, after *QE2's* retirement in fall 2008] and then only from time to time. Car floats are rare sights these days; most piers are empty or demolished – collapsing riverward as cleaner harbor waters invite marine life not seen for 200 years to come back and eat their wooden piles. ★ Today, too, virtually all cargo travels in containers and goes to Newark Bay. Gone are the old sounds of the stevedores, the waterfront bars, the sailors, and the rough sets that depended on them. ★ But as increasingly known to New Yorkers ... ours remains a working harbor, with working vessels, active shipyards, busy ferries and new waterfront access, and hard-working tugs with barges – as well as oil depots and container ports active around the clock.

– *HarborGuide, Working Harbor Committee*

★ HARBOR DISCOVERIES ★

Harbor Discoveries Today – Checklist of Selected Places

From spring through fall each year, the Working Harbor Committee takes all comers out to explore New York harbor by boat. From the container ports and tug yards of New Jersey and Staten Island . . . to Brooklyn's beautiful brick warehouses in Erie and Atlantic basins, and to the Brooklyn Navy Yard . . . to the Hudson Piers and the harbor's centerpiece Ellis, Liberty, and Governors islands and more – limitless behind-the-scenes places are the subject of expert narration and personal discovery from the Working Harbor Committee's Hidden Harbor Tours, about this city that came from the sea. Here are some favorite places from the Working Harbor Committee's celebratory seasonal tours, with an invitation to seek out more.

Staten Island/New Jersey

The Battery – A large park at the southern tip of Manhattan. It is from here that the tide tables used by mariners to predict low and high water begin. Ferries leave here for Statue of Liberty and Ellis Island.

Robbins Reef Lighthouse – The original stone lighthouse was built in 1883, replaced by the current cast iron one in 1933, automated in 1966. The light's most famous Keeper

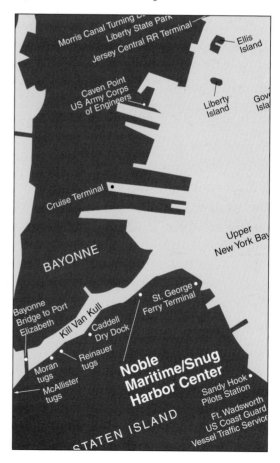

Ship timbers and wildflowers, Shooter's Island.

was widow Kate Walker. From 1886 to 1919, she kept the light burning and also raised two children, rowing them to school on Staten Island every day.

Kill Van Kull – Industrial core of today's working harbor. This narrow waterway between Staten Island and Bayonne, NJ, handles all the container ships and car carriers bound for Newark Bay, and all other traffic bound for the Arthur Kill. The Kill is currently being dredged to accommodate a new, larger class of container ship.

Along the Kill Van Kull – Look for several tug yards – Reinauer Transportation, Moran, McAllister to name a few. In the days of steam,

docking a large ship required up to eight tugs. Commands by the docking pilot were given and acknowledged by a series of whistle signals, still used occasionally today. Modern diesel tugs are much more powerful and fewer are required. . . . Tugs perform all sorts of functions – among them pushing barges, towing barges, and with barges "on the hip" (made up alongside), and ship docking. . . . Caddell Ship Dry Dock and

Repair Company has multiple "dry docks" – large floating open-ended vessels that can be flooded and sunk; a ship is then moved into its center and the dry dock is pumped out and refloated, allowing work on the ship.

Snug Harbor Cultural Center – Inland from the ferry dock lies the entrance to what was Sailor's Snug Harbor, once the largest home in the world for "aged, decrepit and worn-out sailors" (over 1,000 at one time). It's now home to various cultural groups including the Noble Maritime Collection, and is the repository for

Sailors Snug Harbor, SI

the history of Sailor's Snug Harbor. Built between 1831 and the 1880s, it is a National Historic Landmark comprising a series of striking Greek Revival pavilions.

★ ★ ★

Brooklyn/East River

Fulton Ferry Landing – The first ferry started here in 1642; Robert Fulton's (as in Fulton Streets Brooklyn & Manhattan) steam-powered ferry

Verrazano-Narrows Bridge in partial completion, 1963, and stretching to Staten Island, 2008.

service started in 1814. The fireboat house with hose-drying tower was built 1926; the last fireboat was stationed there in 1970. Today, the famous Brooklyn Ice Cream Factory is stationed inside the fireboat house, serving tourists and savvy kids who drag their parents in from all over Brooklyn and Lower Manhattan. On the north side of the landing, yellow New York Water Taxis chug in and out; on the south side, BargeMusic, a floating concert hall, recently celebrated its 30th anniversary at the site.

Brooklyn Bridge – The world's longest suspension bridge when finished in 1883, and thought by many to be the most beautiful to this day. One of

East River's Hell-Gate, 1841

Hell-gate is as pacific at low water as any other stream; as the tide rises, it begins to fret; at half tide it rages and roars, as if bellowing for more water; but when the tide is full, it relapses again into quiet, and for a time seems to sleep almost as soundly as an alderman after dinner. – Washington Irving, 1841, from *New-York Mirror*

the world's engineering marvels, it rests on giant timber caissons 80 feet below the surface. The bottom of the deck is close to 133 feet from the water at high tide, which was the height needed for sailing ships to pass below. Big square-riggers, however, still had to send down their upper spars to fit beneath it. Today, Brooklyn-Manhattan walkers enjoy its pedestrian walkways.

Empire Stores Warehouses – Abandoned decades ago and rendered iconic by photographer Berenice

"Crossing the Brooklyn Bridge under a threatening sky, the World Trade Center rising bright in the background, April 1985."

★ HARBOR DISCOVERIES ★

Abbott, now planned for cultural and commercial life within the new Brooklyn Bridge Park. Built 1870 and 1885; similar warehouses for water-borne freight lined this waterfront south to Red Hook.

Brooklyn Navy Yard – The site of shipyards ever since the English ran things before the Revolution. The Navy bought it in 1801 and departed in 1966, leaving several important Greek Revival style houses. The Navy Yard is now leased to private industry. The oldest graving dock (#1), on the south side, was built in 1840 and still works. Battleships built here include the *Maine* of

Spanish-American war fame, *Arizona,* now a memorial on the bottom of Pearl Harbor, and *Missouri,* aboard which Japan surrendered in Tokyo Bay at the end of World War II. During the war, 71,000 people worked in the Brooklyn Navy Yard.

Atlantic Basin, Red Hook – Completed in 1847, to transfer cargo between ships, warehouses, and canal boats. NYC boomed in the 19th century thanks to trade with the rest of the country via the Erie Canal system. Goods produced in the West arrived here, were processed, and then transferred to vessels headed for the East Coast and the rest of the world. Today the home of Brooklyn's only container terminal and large break-bulk port, American Stevedoring, and where much of the chocolate and lumber we consume arrives. Atlantic Basin is also the New York home of Cunard's *Queen Mary 2,* too large to fit into the West Side's Manhattan Cruise Terminal. Billed as "the largest, longest, tallest, and most expensive ocean liner in the world," she is 1,132 feet long and carries 2,600 passengers.

Harbor Fishing, 1835

Fishing was very good between Blackwell's [Roosevelt] Island and Manhattan, particularly for lobsters. Generally we went directly across the river to Newtown Creek, a pretty, clear stream, very unlike what it is now – good bass in the season with crabs galore.
– Sturtevant, 1835, from *New-York Mirror*

★ HARBOR DISCOVERIES ★

Upper Harbor & the Hudson

Governors Island

With the transfer of Governors Island to NY State and City in 2003, the Governors Island Preservation and Education Corporation was charged with creating new civic spaces with educational, historical, artistic, cultural, and other public-benefit uses that honor the verdant island's history and harbor setting. Strategically located between Lower Manhattan and Brooklyn at the mouth of the East River, the island was home to the Colonial Governor of New York after 1698 and served as a military base for over 200 years. ★ Today, the Governors Island National Monument includes two historic forts and 52

Castle William . . . Ellis Island . . . Liberty Island.

landmarked buildings. The north end tower is a ventilator for Brooklyn-Battery Tunnel – longest vehicular tunnel in the City. Circular Castle William, construction completed nearly two centuries ago, lies along its northwestern shore opposite its counterpart Castle Clinton in Lower Manhattan. ★ Among notable historic events: Wilbur Wright took off from Governors Island and flew over American waters for the first time in

★ HARBOR DISCOVERIES ★

Pier A – Good News!

The restoration of Pier A, the handsome 1895 fireboat pier tucked into the tip of Lower Manhattan, now has new momentum after long delays. With the redevelopment of this elegant Victorian structure now under the aegis of the Battery Park City Authority, Pier A will be reborn in a few years as a bustling ferry hub. Tenants

under consideration for the landmark building with an antique clock tower that chimes the time in ship's bells include shops, a restaurant, a cultural facility, and the National Park Service, which is expected to create a new gateway for travelers to Liberty and Ellis islands. ★ For some fascinating New York marine fire department history details, see www.marine1fdny.com/history.php.

1909. ★ Among newest plans: a major new park, hundreds more trees, and public spaces for performance and recreation. New in 2008: Yankee Pier restored for historic vessels; NY Harbor School confirms its 2010 move on-island; bicyclists can now explore miles of car-free roads and paths. ★ Latest details – www.govisland.com.

Hudson River Park – Now completing construction, borders Manhattan's entire North River (Hudson) waterfront from Battery Park to West 59th Street. Its mixed uses will include recreation, outdoor space, working piers (the Manhattan

Cruise Terminal), mixed-use piers (40 and 57), historic ship piers (25, 54, and 97) and museums (the aircraft carrier Intrepid Sea*Air*Space Museum). The park, which also includes several public access recreational piers, is being built and managed by the Hudson River Park Trust, a joint City-State agency. Pier 84 in the park is the home of the annual Great North River Tugboat Race & Competition.

★ HARBOR DISCOVERIES ★

Battery Park City – Like the rest of the North River in Manhattan, this site was once filled with working piers. Now a shore lined with residential and commercial buildings, it proved its worth on 11 September 2001 when scores of tugs, pilot boats, ferries, and even historic vessels took countless people out of harm's way from its promenade and South Cove. North Cove, its protected marina, was intensively used to coordinate the rescue effort and for months thereafter to provide transport to the site for workers and for the families of those lost in the disaster. The area south of Pier 25 was dredged and barges landed there and transported the rubble from the site to the closed landfill at Fresh Kills, Staten Island. In time of crisis, the working watercraft of New York harbor reaffirmed their worth.

The Morris Canal Turning Basin – The body of water just south of the Colgate Clock in Jersey City. Until 1971 the south side was occupied by the Jersey Central and Lehigh Valley railroads. Its passenger ferry terminal has been restored as part of Liberty State Park. Almost the entire south side and much of the north side is now host to pleasure boats. The Morris Canal takes its name from the original 1825 canal that ran from just inland near the Clock across northern New Jersey to the Delaware River at Phillipsburg.

The Colgate Clock – Preserved even though the factory once below it is long gone. Vessels commonly report their position to one another by radio as being "Southbound at The Clock."

Manhattan Cruise Terminal – After the transatlantic passenger ship trade virtually vanished in the 1960s, Piers 88, 90, and 92 were rebuilt in the 1970s for the cruise ship business and are today over capacity with these thriving enterprises. Details, Jonathan Atkin's industry update, 91.

★ ★ ★

Thank you, on behalf of my teachers & my economics class, for taking time out of your busy schedule to spend time with us, and explain to us how the port business actually works. . . . One thing I learned was, the long and serious process the merchandise goes through before it gets to the store.

– Thanks from a Bronx Community HS student to Lucy Ambrosino, Port Authority of NY/NJ, for her presentation for the Working Harbor Committee on the harbor's importance to both local and global economies

New York Harbor Portfolio

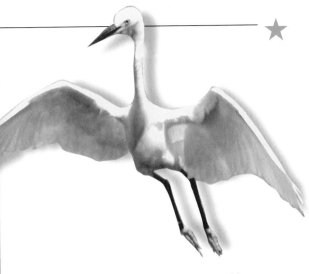

From brisk morning tug-runs to container ship arrivals and kayak forays and liner departures at dusk . . . and celebratory fireworks illuminating our skyline at night . . . favorite photographs by Working Harbor Committee member and professional photographer Bernard Ente.

The Staten Island Ferry was once owned by the Baltimore & Ohio Railroad;
it has been a city service since 1905.

★

The prominent fort on Governors Island is Castle Williams, built in 1811
(along with Castle Clinton at the Battery) to prevent a repeat of the disastrous
British occupation of New York during the Revolution.

★

The Port of New York and New Jersey is the number one handler of automobiles in the U.S. Last year
the port handled over 588,000 autos – traditionally carried in RoRo (Roll-on, Roll-off) ships.

★

Kill Van Kull and Arthur Kill, to the south, are the two waterways that make Staten Island an island.

★

The East River is named not for its relation to Manhattan, but for the direction a ship
is ultimately headed – eastward out toward Long Island Sound. Likewise, mariners call the lower
Hudson River by its old name – the North River, acknowledging a northern river vs the
Delaware River, the "South River," as originally designated by the Dutch.

★

The Williamsburg Bridge opened in 1903 and is named after the Brooklyn neighborhood in which
it lands. When completed, one harbor captain notes, the bridge was considered so ugly that the city
created a City Art Commission to review all public works "to be sure it did not happen again."

★

Manhattan's North River piers are numbered from south to north. Subtracting 40 from the
pier number will give you the closest corresponding street number. Pier 40 is at Houston Street
(near the beginning of numbered streets).

★

The most common exports from New York Harbor are scrap metal and paper.

– *Capt. John Doswell, Working Harbor Committee*

Harbor Highlights Exploration List

Want to know more about New York harbor? The sources are many and varied.
Here are some selected ideas worthy of exploration . . .

American Merchant Marine Museum at Kings Point – created at Long Island's noted United States Merchant Marine Academy, to encourage public interest in our country's merchant marine and to gather and exhibit ship models, paintings, and other historic items reflecting its seafaring heritage. ★ Visitors are welcome, water's edge grounds are beautiful, and glimpsing the Academy is fascinating. ★ *www.usmma.edu*

★

Downtown Boathouse – provides access to the Hudson River for all, via free programs including walk-up public kayaking, kayak trips on the harbor, evening classes, and a winter swimming pool program. ★ In the last decade 100,000+ different people have taken 250,000 Downtown Boathouse trips on the Hudson. ★ *www.downtownboathouse.org*

★

Fireboat *John J. Harvey* – built in 1931, 130-foot MV *John J. Harvey* is among the most powerful fireboats ever in service: five 600 hp diesels and 18,000 gpm pumping capacity. Her pumps are powerful: when she and the George Washington Bridge were both brand new, she shot water over the bridge's roadway. ★ Retired by NYC Fire Department in 1994, bought by current owners in 1999, placed on The National Register in 2000. *Harvey* and her volunteer crew per-

formed heroic rescue work at the World Trade Center on 9/11/01, and today conduct educational tours of harbor and Hudson. Details, page 53 ★ *www.fireboat.org*

★

Floating the Apple – group of NY and NJ residents whose goal is restoring universal access to public waterways; immediate objective – reintroduce the public, especially young people, to the joys of rowing and sailing on urban waters. ★ Seeks to connect city neighborhoods by water with each other and with towns up the rivers, through an informal network of boathouse communities. ★ *www.floatingtheapple.org*

★

Fort Schuyler Maritime Museum – part of the Maritime College of the State University of New York, in the Bronx at Throgs Neck Bridge, with the handsome 152-year-old fort in active use today. Collections include models, paintings, documents, flags, and memorabilia from steamship lines and related maritime industries. ★ No fewer than 700 gleaming ship models, and exquisite maritime paintings, posters, photographs. ★ *www.sunymaritime.edu*

★

Fort Wadsworth, Staten Island – currently, home of U.S. Coast Guard and U.S. Department of Homeland Security – Sector NY. Among services: maritime security/law enforcement, anti-terrorism protection, waterways management, vessel traffic system (VTS), and coordinating recreational boating safety. ★ VTS monitors movements of 360,000+ vessels in the port each year plus 60 million passengers on commuter ferries. ★ Visitors take Ranger-led tours of Battery Weed and Fort Tomkins. ★ *www.nps.gov/gate*

Gateway National Parks of NY Harbor – three separate sites (Staten Island, Jamaica Bay, Sandy Hook) offer diverse recreations and explorations, from swimming-boating-fishing to team sports, bicycling, and nature study. ★ New Jersey's Sandy Hook Lighthouse is the nation's oldest operating lighthouse (1764). ★ Brooklyn-Queens Jamaica Bay Wildlife Refuge coexists with nearby Kennedy Airport. ★ Staten Island's Fort Wadsworth (the unit also includes World War Veterans Park at Miller Field and Great Kills) – see above. ★ *www.nps.gov/gate*

Governors Island – see details (page 167) in Harbor Discoveries list. Check progress in plans for new park with generous public spaces for performance and recreation including car-free paths for bicyclists and pedestrians. ★ *www.govisland.com*

Gowanus Dredgers Canoe Club – volunteer group encouraging public waterfront access and education, and running programs on the shorelines of Gowanus, Red Hook, and DUMBO ("Down Under Manhattan and Brooklyn Bridges"). Goal – as people experience the waterfront through Gowanus Dredgers programs, they become advocates for its revitalization. ★ In a recent season, logged 2,000+ trips on the Gowanus Canal. ★ *www.gowanuscanal.org*

Hudson-Fulton-Champlain Quadricentennial – 2009 marks 400th anniversary of Hudson and Champlain's voyages along the river and lake that bear their names, and 200th anniversary of Fulton's famed Hudson River voyage, with visitors from all over the world. ★ *www.exploreny400.com*

Hudson River Sloop Clearwater – non-profit organization working to defend and restore the Hudson River, its tributaries, and related bodies of water via environmental education and advocacy programs and celebrations. ★ The sloop *Clearwater* herself is a frequent and much admired Hudson River sight. ★ *www.clearwater.org*

Intrepid Sea*Air*Space Museum – a famed WWII aircraft carrier and national historic landmark right in the Hudson River. After the war the U.S.S. *Intrepid* went on to serve as a recovery vessel for NASA, and later into service in Vietnam. Today, planes, submarines, helicopters, interactive exhibits, and public events attract both international tourists and local residents. ★ After extensive refitting in dry dock elsewhere in the port, the *Intrepid* reopens in year-end 2008. Details, page 60 ★ *www.intrepidmuseum.org*

Liberty State Park – a vital waterfront renaissance in the New York harbor area. As railroads and related industry declined, shores were abandoned as desolate sites. Old buildings and overgrown tracks transformed into a modern urban state park opened on Flag Day, June 14, 1976, as New Jersey's bicentennial gift to the nation. ★ Most of this 1,122-acre park is open space with 300 acres developed for public recreation. ★ *www.libertystatepark.org*

★

Metropolitan Waterfront Alliance – works through education, grassroots organizing, and media advocacy to include the public's voice and values in decision-making that will determine the future of our region's waterfront and waterways. ★ Projects include revitalized East River and Hudson waterfronts, harbor transportation, public access, and educational conferences for people who want to make it all happen, with frequent updates on key harbor topics via website and email newsletter WaterwireNews. ★ *www.waterwire.net*

★

National Maritime Historical Society – works to preserve and perpetuate U.S. maritime history and to invite all to share in the challenging heritage of seafaring. ★ NMHS's Sea History Press publications include *Sea History* magazine, distributed nationally to a broad maritime audience. ★ Recent articles: insights of ancient Greek mariners, heroic efforts of World War II seamen, NY harbor paintings by renowned artist John Stobart, and Sea History for Kids section. ★ *www.seahistory.org*

★

Newtown Creek Alliance – formed in 2002 to educate decision-makers about Newtown Creek, end persistent sources of Creek pollution, host community events on and around the Creek, and more. ★ NCA members include elected officials, environmental advocates, community residents, business leaders, Newtown Creek users. ★ Runs frequent sold-out narrated tours; all comers welcome. ★ *www.newtowncreekalliance.org*

★

New York Outrigger & Liberty Challenge Outrigger Canoe Race – helps educate thousands of New Yorkers to be safe and confident paddlers in New York's waterways. ★ Hosts the Liberty World Outrigger Competition in June – 15-mile men's & women's races and an 11-mile mixed race, East River to Hudson River and the Statue of Liberty. ★ *www.newyorkoutrigger.org*

★

Noble Maritime Collection, Staten Island – a maritime museum and study center on the shore of the busy shipping waterway Kill Van Kull. Housed in the famous old home for mariners, Sailors' Snug Harbor. Is dedicated to the life and work of distinguished marine artist John A. Noble (1913-83) and continues his legacy of celebrating the people and traditions of NY harbor. Presents exhibitions on the modern maritime industry, publishes books, and runs an extensive education program for children and adults. In the museum – galleries, library and archive, classrooms, and museum shop; also houses the houseboat studio where Noble did most of his art chronicling the harbor during the

last chapter in the Age of Sail. Details, page 30 ★
www.noblemaritime.org

NY Water Taxi – runs those taxi-yellow vessels connecting neighborhoods and attractions on New York's waterfront. And, offers tours, charters, and special-occasion cruises. ★ Started in 2002 and all over the harbor now, with water the "road" between city places. Details, page 40. ★ *www.nywatertaxi.com*

★

Olga's BargeMusic – retired coffee barge anchored in Brooklyn 30 years ago by classical violinist Olga Bloom, now hosts acclaimed evenings of classical music and jazz concerts. ★ Per a *Daily News* article, "Ms Bloom says 'It's like playing inside a finely made violin, where the walls boast wood scavenged from an old retired Staten Island ferry.'" ★ *www.bargemusic.org*

★

Pier 66 Maritime – former car float (railroad barge) now a lively public access pier at the foot of West 26th Street, Hudson River. Originally used by Delaware, Lackawanna and Western railroad, the floating "pier" now provides waterfront access, docking, kayaking, home to historic vessels, and refreshments with the best view in town. ★ Reopened summer '08 after renovations. Details, page 149 ★ *www.hudsonriverpark.org*

★

PortSide New York – seeks to enhance interconnections of landside communities and the maritime sector to mutual advantage. Chief ambassador in this mission:

the tanker *Mary Whalen,* which once delivered fuel up and down the Atlantic Coast; she went out of service in 1993 and in her new life will house PortSide New York activities such as Tanker Tours, Red Hook Visitors Guide, community sailing, and art programs. ★ *www.portsidenewyork.org*

Schooner *Adirondack* **and Motor Yacht** *Manhattan* – both built by Scarano Boat Works, these elegant vessels offer differing ways to enjoy the harbor: by sail aboard the classic 80-foot pilot schooner *Adirondack,* or on the new '20s-style motor yacht *Manhattan.* Choose group scenic/educational or private-celebration cruises. ★ *www.sail-nyc.com*

★

Shearwater Sailing – elegant 1920s era schooner, resplendent in mahogany and teak, gives day and evening harbor sails for the public and special groups. She served in the Coast Guard Patrol during World War II. ★ On a recent sunset sail, "a giant yellow-red moon rose over one end of the harbor with city lights interconnecting all around, and the Statue of Liberty's crown illuminated from within." ★ *www.shearwatersailing.com*

South Street Seaport Museum – honors the history of the port of New York and its commercial and cultural impact on city, state, and nation. To see: galleries, educational and special events for children and adults, and historic vessels berthed in the East River just south of the Brooklyn Bridge – among them the square-rigger *Wavertree* and *Ambrose* Lightship. ★ Architectural centerpiece – 1812 Schermerhorn Row, within seven-square-block historic district of 19th-century buildings along stone-paved streets. Call ahead for harbor tours aboard historic schooner *Pioneer* or jaunty 1930 tug *W. O. Decker*. ★ *www.southstseaport.org*

★

Statue of Liberty/Ellis Island – on 12-acre mid-harbor Liberty Island, the Statue of Liberty Enlightening the World was a gift of friendship from the people of France to the people of the United States and stands for freedom. Dedicated in 1886, designated a National Monument in 1924, restored for her centennial on July 4, 1986. ★ Nearby Ellis Island – handsome architecture meticulously restored – invites families to share immigration stories with its National Museum of Immigration. ★ *www.nps.gov/stli* and *www.ellisisland.org*

★

Tug Race "Great North River Tugboat Race & Competition" – spectacular Hudson River Labor Day Sunday event attracts tugs of all kinds and sizes from the 7,000 hp *Lincoln Sea*, race winner overall in 2006, to the tiny historic *W. O. Decker* from South Street Seaport Museum. ★ The day starts with a tug parade with whistles and bells, fireboats spraying, 79th to 44th Street race, then bow-to-bow pushing and line tosses to a bollard on Pier 84. ★ Tug *Lucy Reinauer* won for '07, against 17 competitors in the 15th annual race, amid cheers of all public present. The Working Harbor Committee's spectator vessel followed the race downriver. Details, page 95. ★ *www.workingharbor.org*

★

Waterfront Museum and Showboat Barge – restored railroad barge *Lehigh Valley No. 79* is today a floating museum at Pier 44, Brooklyn, promoting waterfront access and historic preservation. ★ Public events include Circus Sundays, a music series, and ongoing maritime education programs on NY harbor as a waterway for commerce and commuters as well as culture and recreation. ★ *www.waterfrontmuseum.org*

★

Working Harbor Committee – offers modestly priced Working Harbor Day boat tours to behind-the-scenes places all around the harbor in May, Hidden Harbor Tours in summer and fall, and The Great North River Tugboat Race & Competition (see above) on Labor Day Sunday. In seasonal harbor-education programs, introduces high school students to the maritime industry and prospective careers within it. ★ Tour narrators are selected for intriguing backgrounds, know the harbor inside and out, and tell stories you'll hear nowhere else. Working Harbor Day details – see page 151. ★ *www.workingharbor.org*

*– Compiled by Capt. John Doswell,
Working Harbor Committee*

NOTE – A well-worth-reading blog about "New York harbor – the sixth borough" – is www.tugster.wordpress.com. Great harbor photographs!

Harbor Voices Authors, Photographers, Artists, & Sources

Terry Walton is a lifelong sailor, former managing editor of *Boating* magazine, the founding editor of *Seaport* magazine, and a founding trustee of South Street Seaport Museum. She is a maritime editor and vice chair of the Working Harbor Committee and has written about New York harbor adventures for 30 years. Her parents met thanks to her father crewing on the square-rigger *Tusitala*. She and her husband sailed their 28-foot Herreshoff ketch in and around Long Island for 22 years with their two children.

Norman Brouwer is a maritime historian, researcher, author, and former merchant seaman. He wrote extensively for South Street Seaport Museum's *Seaport* Magazine, and spent many years as SSSM curator and acting librarian. He is editor of the standard work *International Register of Historic Ships.*

Capt. John Doswell is executive director of the Working Harbor Committee and a founder of Friends of Hudson River Park. He created WHC's Hidden Harbor Tours© program and serves on the boards of diverse waterfront organizations.

Bernard Ente is a professional photographer and a leading member of the Working Harbor Committee. His photographs of the working harbor's waterways, vessels, railroads, and bridges have been widely published. He frequently hosts sell-out Hidden Harbor Tours for WHC.

Peter Stanford is the founder of South Street Seaport Museum, president emeritus of the National Maritime Historical Society, and editor at large of the Society's *Sea History* magazine. He is a much-published maritime writer and the founding chair of the Working Harbor Committee. Among his projects nearing completion – a book on the founding years of the Seaport Museum.

With Thanks –

Grateful acknowledgement is here given to South Street Seaport Museum for permission to reprint copyrighted articles from the South Street *Reporter* and *Seaport* magazine; to *Seaport* magazine's early photographers who said "yes!" when I asked to use their photographs decades after their first printing; and to the Working Harbor Committee and its authors and photographers for extracts from *HarborGuide*. ★ I give special thanks to the following individuals and sources, for permission to include new or reprinted material as noted: William F. Baker, Steven Bendo, Bill Bleyer, Chris Bowser, Ann Buttenweiser, Sabato "Sal" Catucci, Bob Davidson, James Devine, Jessica DuLong, Michael Fairchild, Murray Fisher, Capt. Timothy J. Ferrie, Capt. Thomas F. Fox, Tom Fox, David Fuchs, Ben Gibberd, Edmund V. Gillon Jr, Capt. Huntley Gill, Lee Gruzen, Capt. Pamela Hepburn, Capt. Glenn Hodgdon, Steven P. Kalil, Hope Killcoyne, John and Angela Krevey, Henrik Krogius, Julie Laudicina, Capt. Geo Matteson, Capt. Brian McAllister, James McGeehan, John Mylod,

Minda Novek, Alan Orling, Jeff Perkell,
Capt. George Previll, Eric Proctor, Jack Putnam,
Naima Rauam, Capt. Cynthia Robson,
Ellen Fletcher Russell, John Senzer,
Capt. Bill Sherwood, Alison Simko, Richard Stepler,
RADM Doug Teeson, USCG, Marty Umans,
Erin Urban, John Waldman, Jenifer Walton,
Jerome Zukosky

South Street Seaport Museum –
   Reporter and *Seaport* magazines; book *Pioneer Lives*
Working Harbor Committee –
   HarborGuides 2001–2006

———————

Collection of Brooklyn Historical Society
Collection of Chris Reinauer, Reinauer Transportation
Collection of Frank Braynard, *A Tugman's Sketchbook*
Collection of Naima Rauam
Collection of New-York Historical Society*
Collection of New York Public Library*
Collection of Noble Maritime
Collection of Mystic Seaport*
Collection of Norman Brouwer
Collection of Port Captain Steven Bendo
Collection of The University of Louisville*
Customs and Border Control photography archives, by
   Jim Tourtelotte
Globe Pequot Press, *New York Waters,* by Ben Gibberd
Intrepid Sea*Air*Space Museum photography archives

Lyons Press, *Heartbeats in the Muck,* by John Waldman
The Marine Society of the City of New York
Metropolitan Waterfront Alliance
The Millay Society
National Maritime Historical Society –
   Sea History Magazine
New York University Press, *Tugboats of New York,*
   by Geo Matteson
New York *Daily News* Archives
Sail Magazine

———————

* *Special Permissions*

Cover – New York Harbor 1860; #57699,
collection of the New-York Historical Society

Page vi – Ship Tusitala, c Mystic Seaport,
Rosenfeld Collection, Mystic, CT; #16962F;
www.rosenfeldcollection.org ~
rosenfeld@mysticseaport.org

Page 132 – Customs House, photographer Todd
Webb, U.S. Customs Station at foot of Hamilton
Street, South Brooklyn, March 1947; #45331, collec-
tion of the University of Louisville

Page 136 – Lackawanna Ferry Terminal, Berenice
Abbott; #482554, Ferry, West 23rd Street, Manhattan,
1935; Photography Collection, Miriam and Ira D.
Wallach Division of Art, Prints and Photographs,
The New York Public Library, Astor, Lenox and
Tilden Foundations

★ ★ ★ ★ ★